Introvert
by Design

Other Works by Holley Gerth

You're Already Amazing
You're Made for a God-Sized Dream
You're Going to Be Okay
What Your Heart Needs for the Hard Days
You're Loved No Matter What
Fiercehearted
Hope Your Heart Needs
Strong, Brave, Loved
The Powerful Purpose of Introverts
What Your Soul Needs for Stressful Times
What Your Mind Needs for Anxious Moments

Introvert by Design

A Guided Journal for Living with

New Confidence in

Who You're Created to Be

Holley Gerth

Revell

a division of Baker Publishing Group
Grand Rapids, Michigan

Published by Revell
a division of Baker Publishing Group
Grand Rapids, Michigan 49516-6287
www.revellbooks.com

Printed in the United States of America

Library of Congress Cataloging-in-Publication Data
Names: Gerth, Holley, author.
Title: Introvert by design : a guided journal for living with new confidence in who you're created to be / Holley Gerth.
Description: Grand Rapids, MI : Revell, a division of Baker Publishing Group, [2023] | Includes bibliographical references.
Identifiers: LCCN 2022033210 | ISBN 9780800742805 (paperback) | ISBN 9781493442072 (ebook)
Subjects: LCSH: Introversion—Religious aspects—Christianity. | Introverts—Religious life. | Spiritual journals—Authorship.
Classification: LCC BV4597.58.I58 G465 2023 | DDC 155.2/32—dc23/eng/20221011
LC record available at https://lccn.loc.gov/2022033210

Interior design by William Overbeeke.
Illustrations by Olivia Stallmer.

23 24 25 26 27 28 29   7 6 5 4 3 2 1

contents

introduction

introvert, God created you on purpose

In the beginning, God created pink flamingos and orange starfish, the bitterness of grapefruit and sweetness of honey, the thrill of sex and stillness of sleep, the smell of rainstorms and sound of laughter. He created the heavens and earth, land and sea, masculine and feminine. He is a God of contrast and complements. And I believe, from the very start, he intentionally designed introverts and extroverts too.

Maybe that's not what you've been told. You've probably heard "you're too quiet." You might have been pressured to change by a boss, a peer, or even a family member. In your lowest moments, you might have even wondered if God made a mistake when he crafted you. I'm here to tell you the opposite—you are a wonder, a miracle, the art and joy of a God who built you for moments of silence and deep thinking, for meaningful relationships and restorative work, for showing this world the power of a nurtured soul.

What have you heard as an introvert (example: "You're too quiet")?

What's a different way to see it (example: God designed me to listen well)?

I've been told . . .

A different way to see it is . . .

What proof do I have that you're created as an introvert? We now live in an age of technology where we can literally see into our minds. And what researchers keep finding is that introverts and extroverts are wired in unique ways. For example, we rely on different primary neurotransmitters, parts of our nervous system, and even brain pathways for processing. I'll go deeper into all these later. For now, what you most need to know is that when God dreamed you into being, he knew you'd be an introvert.

When we try to live as someone we're not, we drift from God's divine image in us. I found this out the hard way by pushing myself to the brink of burnout trying to be an extrovert because I believed that was what was required. I bent my true self into the shape I thought everyone wanted, and it broke me. It has taken years for me to heal, to come back home to who I really am, to grow quietly comfortable in my own skin. I never want anyone else to go through what I did.

"Then God looked over all he had made, and he saw that it was *very good!*" (GEN. 1:31)

Look at the story of creation and know you are part of it. Look at history and know you are here for such a time as this. Look at yourself and dare to say that what God made is good.

It's time to trade the insecurities you've felt about being an introvert for new confidence in who you're created to be, starting right now.

How to Use the Guided Journaling Space

Transformation doesn't happen by accident; it takes intentionality and action. This guided journal uses a process that will move you toward confidence one simple, doable step at a time. As a coach, counselor, and bestselling author of *The Powerful Purpose of Introverts*, I've designed this journal based on research and what I've seen work for introverts.

Each day will begin with a reading like the one you just finished. Some of this content is totally new, and some of it is curated from the core concepts of my book *The Powerful Purpose of Introverts*. Each reading is followed by interactive journaling sections that will help you:

* Connect in a deeper way with God through solitude and simple prayers.
* Become more aware of what's happening in your inner world.
* Learn to manage what energizes you and drains you as an introvert.
* Develop helpful habits like reflection, gratitude, and taking the next small step.

* Live each day as an introvert in ways that allow you to thrive and serve.

The guided journaling space has three sections: In This Moment, Yesterday, and Today. Let's walk through them together so you're ready to start using them when you get to day one of the journal. If you need a reminder of how to use the guided journaling space once you get started, you can come back to these pages.

Section 1: In This Moment

Because our minds are so active, introverts often get pulled into mistakes of the past or concerns about the future. So each day's journaling starts with being present *in this moment*.

One simple way to bring our attention to this moment is with a *breath prayer*, which is simply a short prayer that is an affirmation of truth. As introverts, we can struggle with believing lies about who we are, so it's important that we realign with our true identity each day.

God's name is not "I was."

It's not "I will be."

His name is "I am."

This present moment is where we can most fully connect with him.

As introverts, we also need simple ways to calm our bodies and quiet our minds (we'll talk more specifically about why later).

As you say the breath prayer for each day of the journal, remember to:

* Take a deep breath in through your nose.
* Hold your breath for a count of three.
* Release your breath slowly through your mouth.
* Hold your lungs empty for a count of three.
* Repeat the prayer and breathing until you feel calm.

After the breath prayer, you'll have a practical application or question to ponder that will help you engage in a deeper way with what you've read that day.

The *In This Moment* section closes with a quote, usually from a fellow introvert, that offers an insight or helpful perspective.

Section 2: Yesterday

Introverts excel at reflection. While we don't want to get stuck in the past, we do want to intentionally learn from it. The *Yesterday* section will help you do so in two important ways.

First, one of the most essential elements of thriving as an introvert is energy management. If we're not aware of how what's happening in our lives impacts us, we're headed for exhaustion and burnout. This section will give you a simple prompt to help you learn what fills you up and what drains you.

The goal of this exercise isn't to never have moments that drain you. That's not only impossible, but it would also deprive you of some of life's most rewarding experiences. What matters is that you manage what drains you so it doesn't become the master of you.

The more filled up you are, the more you can pour out to others. Knowing what you need as an introvert and honoring that isn't selfish; it's preparation for service.

When you discover something that fills you up as an introvert, you can ask . . .

How can I have more of this in my life?

When you find something that drains you, you can ask . . .

Can I eliminate this from my life?
If not, can I delegate it?
If not, can I minimize it?
If not, what strategies will help me through it?

One thing that can be draining to introverts is our tendency to feel like we're not doing enough. Our brains have a negativity bias (more on that later), so our perceptions of how well we're doing and what we're accomplishing are often inaccurate.

Second, to counter that kind of thinking, you'll make a Ta-Da! List each day that encourages you to look back and record three things you did the day before and celebrate them—*nothing is too small to write down.*

Section 3: Today

After you focus and reflect, you'll be ready to prepare for the day. You'll do so in three simple but effective ways: releasing worries, practicing gratitude, and making a doable plan.

As introverts, we can get stuck in rumination—which is a fancy name for worries on repeat in our minds. Research has shown it helps to get those worries out of our minds and onto paper. When you capture a worry, you can give it to God and ask for his help.

It's not enough just to release our worries. We need to replace them. Research has also shown gratitude shifts our perspective and primes our minds to look for what's good and helpful in our lives. Making gratitude a habit can impact our mental health and overall well-being as introverts.

As the final part of this section, you'll create a "Do What You Can" Plan for the day. Introverts are great at imagining what could be, coming up with big plans, and setting high expectations. This can mean we never actually take small steps toward our goals or dreams.

Your "Do What You Can" Plan will help you prioritize steady growth and progress over perfection. What are three small things you can realistically get done today?

Section 4: Thoughts, Feelings, All the Things

Your inner world as an introvert is full of thinking, feeling, dreaming, learning, observing, exploring, pondering, processing, and imagining.

This final section provides blank space for you to capture whatever is happening inside you. *As you move forward, remember...*

This journey is paved with GRACE, not GUILT.
It's about steady PROGRESS, not PERFECTION.
It's a gentle INVITATION, not an OBLIGATION.

There is no right or wrong way to do the exercises in the guided journaling sections. Make them work for *you*. This is your space, and you can use it however you feel is most helpful.

If you miss a day, it's okay. Go at the pace you need and give yourself room to process. If you get distracted or busy, just pick up where you left off and keep going.

As an introvert, you're likely hard on yourself. As you go through this process, speak to yourself as you would someone you love.

No matter how you feel on any given day, no matter what you do or don't do, this is still true: *you're enough, you're already loved, and you're gifted with strengths our world needs more than ever before.*

Let's get started.

Visit HolleyGerth.com/Introverts
for even more introvert resources.

one

embrace the gift
of solitude

Have you ever stood in a crowded room and felt alone?

I'm at an event holding a tiny plate covered with crackers and cheese, green grapes, and a few olives, wondering how to eat without looking awkward. Actually, I'm wondering how to even *be* in this room without awkwardness. All around me conversations flow, laughter echoes, and people exchange contact information, but I feel out of place.

One of the biggest myths in our world today is that isolation is about physical space. If someone is in a room by themselves, they must be isolated. If they're in a room full of other people, they must be connected. But we, as introverts, know deep down it doesn't really work that way.

What's a time when you felt alone even when you were with people? What's a time when you didn't feel alone even though you were physically by yourself?

On every day of creation, God pronounced what he made good. Then he said, "It is not good for the man to be alone" (Gen. 2:18). The word *alone* in this verse isn't about our proximity to others; it's about the level of intimacy in our lives. The original meaning of *alone* in this context essentially expresses *living disconnected from God, others, and our true selves.*

In contrast, solitude is time when we're physically apart from others for a specific purpose like prayer, creative work, reflection, a walk outside in nature, or going through this journal. Isolation is draining; solitude is restorative.

3 Things I Enjoy Doing in Solitude

1.

2.

3.

For most of the church's history, solitude was seen as an important spiritual discipline. Breaks from the outside world were viewed as essential for the soul, and even

"Jesus often *withdrew* to the *wilderness* for prayer" (LUKE 5:16).

As introverts, we can shame ourselves for our need to have time alone. We might tell ourselves it's an indulgent luxury when so many people and tasks demand our attention. But what if our need for time alone is actually *holy*? What if it was placed there by a God who values quiet just as much as boldness, who invites us into stillness and not just busy schedules, who offers restoration and inspiration in the moments no one else is around?

Our noisy, chaotic world needs people with the courage to choose solitude. It helps all of us to reflect rather than react, to be intentional instead of impulsive, to live filled up rather than stressed out. It gives us room to create, dream, innovate. Our greatest contributions to others are likely to flow from solitude. By practicing it, we give those around us permission to slow their pace, lower their volume, and reconnect to what matters most.

I walk outside of the conference into a cloudless, silent evening. The stars are flung across the sky, diamonds on velvet. I remember I'm part of something so much bigger than I am, that I belong to Someone who spoke all this into being, that he is with me even now.

Solitude is not selfish; it's a sacred invitation.

Solitude is not selfish; it's a sacred invitation.

IN THIS MOMENT

Please refer back to the *How to Use the Guided Journaling Space* section in the introduction if you need a reminder about how to use these sections.

BREATH PRAYER:
God, you are always with me whether
I am with others or alone.

Solitude often takes intentional planning. Pause and choose a time for solitude this week. Schedule it just like you would an important meeting. When and where will you have solitude?

_____

_____

_____

_____

_____

_____

For an introvert like me, being alone for any amount of time recharges me. In the midst of a busy day I'll sit in my car for a few extra minutes before coming inside just to enjoy a few minutes of rest or silence before jumping into whatever's next.

—JOANNA GAINES

yesterday

A moment that filled me up was . . .

A moment that drained me was . . .

TA–DA! LIST

1. _____

2. _____

3. _____

today

One thing I'm worried about today is . . .

One thing I'm grateful for today is . . .

MY "DO WHAT YOU CAN" PLAN

1. _____

2. _____

3. _____

thoughts, feelings, ALL THE THINGS

two

enjoy meaningful relationships

Search for introvert memes, and you'll quickly find this one: "Introverts Unite (Separately in Your Own Homes)." It makes me laugh but also spreads a common misconception about introverts—that we somehow love people less than extroverts do. The truth? Introverts love people just as much as extroverts; we just do so in different ways.

An extrovert might enjoy a dinner party with a dozen people around the table, while an introvert likely prefers coffee with one friend. Why? Because as introverts, we're built to go deep rather than wide.

> AS INTROVERTS, WE'RE BUILT TO GO *deep* RATHER THAN *wide*.

One reason for this is the primary neurotransmitter we rely on. Extroverts prefer dopamine, which is released in high-stimulation situations (like that twelve-person dinner party). Introverts thrive on acetylcholine, which is released when we're able to fully focus, whether on a project we're passionate about, personal reflection, or a meaningful conversation with one person.

I did a survey asking my subscribers, "Are you an introvert or extrovert?" and "What's your biggest challenge as an introvert or extrovert?"

What's your biggest challenge as an introvert?

To my surprise, the most common answer for extroverts was *loneliness*. They said things like, "I have a lot of acquaintances, but I long for deeper connections." Introvert, your style of socializing is needed in this world—especially by the people who look like they have plenty of connections.

All through the New Testament, the phrase *"one another"* is repeated.

* "Love one another" (JOHN 13:34 NIV).

* "Accept one another" (ROM. 15:7 NIV).

* "Encourage one another" (2 COR. 13:11 NIV).

* "Serve one another" (GAL. 5:13 NIV).

* "Be kind and compassionate to one another" (EPH. 4:32 NIV).

These verses don't say "love groups of people" or "love everyone at once." They say *one* another. Your introvert preference for connecting with people one-on-one is not a weakness, it's a God-given *strength*.

When an expert in the law asked Jesus what mattered most, his answer was to love God and "love your neighbor as yourself'" (Luke 10:27). He didn't say love your neighbors (plural); he said love your neighbor (singular). Then he told the story of the good Samaritan, which is about one person helping another.

When it comes to relationships, *quality over quantity* is the theme. It's not about *how many* people we have in our lives but *how well* we love whoever God puts in front of us each day.

Who is one person you can love today? What's one way you can do so?

So let's release any expectations we have of ourselves about how many friends we make, the frequency of social events on our calendar, or the number of likes we get on social media. Instead, let's focus on loving others in the powerful way God designed us to—one person at a time.

IN THIS MOMENT

BREATH PRAYER:
*God, I am loved by you, and you will
love others through me today.*

Go back to the list of "one another" phrases and choose one to focus on. Write it below along with a few ideas for how you can live it out today.

You don't need everyone to love you, just a few good people.

—Introvert CHARITY BARNUM to her extrovert
husband in *The Greatest Showman*

yesterday

A moment that filled me up was . . .

A moment that drained me was . . .

TA-DA! LIST

1. _____

2. _____

3. _____

today

One thing I'm worried about today is . . .

One thing I'm grateful for today is . . .

MY "DO WHAT YOU CAN" PLAN

1. _____

2. _____

3. _____

thoughts, feelings, ALL THE THINGS

three

take "you're so quiet" as a compliment

I'm at a retreat, the kind with awkward "tell everyone a little about yourself" introductions, team-building activities, and s'mores around a campfire at night. The latter is actually my favorite time of the day, the only one where I feel I can catch my breath. I'm sitting silently, staring at the stars, listening to the conversations around me. Then a gregarious member of the group approaches me and makes this comment: "You're so quiet!"

Introverts often love quiet. List 3 reasons why you do.
    I love quiet because . . . (example: it helps me feel peaceful, it gives me space to process)

1.

2.

3.

Now try applying those positive qualities of quietness to yourself.

Being a quiet person means . . . (example: I help others feel peaceful, I give others space to process)

1.

2.

3.

"You're so quiet" isn't a new phrase to me. I heard it from elementary school teachers when I got good grades but didn't often raise my hand in class. Well-meaning family members sometimes say it to me at holiday get-togethers. Coworkers have mentioned it in meetings. Even now, when so much of my life is public, I still hear those words in places where people think that just because I write words means I also always love saying them out loud.

Have you ever heard "you're so quiet" too? Maybe you've thought of this phrase like I did—as a criticism, not a compliment. We live in a time when being outspoken is often encouraged, but it hasn't always been that way. Throughout most of history, quiet was valued. As proof, I've rounded up a list of ancient yet still relevant truths that talk about quiet as something positive and powerful.

* "I wait *quietly* before God, for my victory comes from him" (PS. 62:1).

* "I have calmed and *quieted* myself" (PS. 131:2).

* "For everything there is a season. . . . A time to be *quiet* and a time to speak" (ECCLES. 3:1, 7).

* "A *quiet* spirit can overcome even great mistakes" (ECCLES. 10:4).

* "In *quietness* and confidence is your strength" (ISA. 30:15).

* "My people will live in safety, *quietly* at home" (ISA. 32:18).

* "Jesus said, 'Let's go off by ourselves to a *quiet* place and rest awhile'" (MARK 6:31).

* "Make it your goal to live a *quiet* life" (1 THESS. 4:11).

Also, the preference for lots of talking isn't dominant throughout the world. In many cultures, especially Eastern ones, a quiet nature is seen as a sign of wisdom. Introvert children in these cultures are often more popular than their highly outspoken peers.

What does all this mean?

The most powerful thing you can do is embrace your quietness, not change it.

Your quietness is one of the most positive parts of you, not a problem to fix.

Quietness isn't weakness or lack of confidence; embracing silence takes strength, courage, and humility. Often those who talk most are also the most insecure.

Yes, there is a time to speak up. But there are also many times when quiet is exactly what's needed. So next time someone says, "You're so quiet," what if we simply say, "Thank you," then carry on being who we're created to be?

I'm learning this: "You're so quiet" isn't a criticism; it's a compliment.

IN THIS MOMENT

BREATH PRAYER:
God, thank you for the gift of quiet—
may I receive it, may I offer it to others.

Quiet helps us observe and be more aware. Sit in silence for one minute. What can you see, hear, touch, taste, smell?

The quiet ones, the introverts, are uniquely gifted. We have tremendous patience and empathy. We don't need to say much, yet we're able to build deep connections and rapport with those around us.

—JOEL ANNESLEY

yesterday

A moment that filled me up was . . .

A moment that drained me was . . .

TA—DA! LIST

1. _____

_____

2. _____

_____

3. _____

_____

today

One thing I'm worried about today is . . .

One thing I'm grateful for today is . . .

MY "DO WHAT YOU CAN" PLAN

1. _____

_____

2. _____

_____

3. _____

_____

thoughts, feelings, ALL THE THINGS

four

accept who you truly are

When I started publishing books and speaking publicly over a decade ago, I told myself, "Now I have to be an extrovert. It's just part of the job." I pushed myself to the brink of burnout. At the end of a year when I'd traveled far more than was good for me, I sensed God whispering to my heart, "It's time to go home."

> **Expectations lead us away from who we're created to be. What are three expectations you've unintentionally taken on as an introvert (example: I should be talkative)?**
>
> I should be . . .
>
> 1.
>
> 2.
>
> 3.

I knew this meant, yes, go home and take a long nap (I certainly needed one). But I knew he was also saying it was time to go home to who he created me to *be*. I started a long process of healing that included counseling, confiding in supportive friends, changing my schedule, and finding out everything I could about what it really means to be an introvert.

I discovered I'd believed so many myths, like extroverts make better leaders or have more to offer. But the research says otherwise. Study after study shows introverts perform as well and contribute just as much as extroverts. We just do it in our own ways, which are needed more than ever before.

During that season of healing, I thought often of Isaiah 30:15, which says,

"In *quietness* and *confidence*

is your strength."

I'd believed lies like, "in *being more outgoing* and confidence was my strength" or "in *changing who I am* and confidence was my strength." Maybe you've done the same?

How would you fill in these blanks?

In _____ and _____ is my strength.

I want to extend to you the same invitation my heart received years ago: if you feel insecure about who God created you to be, if you've put pressure on yourself to be more like others you admire, if you're worn out and weary from not honoring your own beautiful limits—it's time to go home.

Acceptance begins with recognizing you're already enough. Not simply because of your humanness but because you are a divine masterpiece, dreamed up in God's heart, woven together by his invisible hands, and placed in this world for a purpose.

There has never been and will never be another you. Either we get what you have to offer to the world through you or not at all. There is no Plan B or backup strategy. There is simply *you*—imperfect and fully loved, entrusted with gifts even on the days you can't see them, an extraordinary introvert who is here for such a time as this.

YOU ARE A
DIVINE *masterpiece,*
DREAMED UP
IN GOD'S *heart,*
WOVEN TOGETHER
BY HIS INVISIBLE *hands,*
AND PLACED IN THIS WORLD
FOR A *purpose.*

IN THIS MOMENT

BREATH PRAYER:
God, I release the expectations I've placed
on myself, and I return home to who you made me.

In the empty space inside the house below, write a few words that describe who you truly are—not who others expect you to be.

Accepting who I am has truly led to a transformation for me. I started out as an introvert who felt very misunderstood, apologetic of what I saw as a weakness. And when I grew to understand myself, I saw my personality traits in a different light. A brighter and clearer light.... Self-acceptance made me bolder and braver.

—ANGELA M. WARD

yesterday

today

A moment that filled me up was . . .

One thing I'm worried about today is . . .

A moment that drained me was . . .

One thing I'm grateful for today is . . .

TA—DA! LIST

MY "DO WHAT YOU CAN" PLAN

1. _____

1. _____

2. _____

2. _____

3. _____

3. _____

thoughts, feelings, ALL THE THINGS

five
find your own rhythm

The sun is just coming up over the horizon, and as a former "not a morning person," I'm doing something unexpected—running. I got COVID-19 in early 2021, and while my case was mild, I couldn't run for months. I kept trying to force myself to resume my previous routine, but my body refused. How could I start again in a sustainable way?

I found a training program that used gradually increasing rhythms like walk one minute, run one minute, walk three minutes, run four minutes, walk five minutes, run ten minutes. Before this season in my life, I would hit the trail and keep the same pace the entire time, no matter how tired I became. But what I really needed, what would have served me better even before having COVID-19, were *rhythms*, not routines.

Routines	Rhythms
Rigid	Flexible
Focus on perfection	Focus on progress
Repetitive	Adapt and grow

For an introvert, a routine might sound like, "I have to show up to every holiday gathering and stay the entire time." A rhythm sounds like, "I'll intentionally choose a few gatherings and go home when I'm ready to rest." Or "I must force myself to be 'on' every moment I'm at work" instead of "I'll use my social energy in the important meeting coming up, then find a quiet place to work for the rest of the day."

With faith, a routine might sound like, "I have to connect with God only in group settings, like worship services and Bible studies." A rhythm sounds like, "I value community, but I'll also remember to include restorative spiritual disciplines like solitude and quiet reflection." *Run, walk, run, walk, run, walk.*

> **What's a routine you've tried to force yourself to have?**
> **What's a rhythm that might better fit who you are as an introvert?**

As a runner, I've started falling in love with rhythms because I've realized this: while they don't make me faster, they do help me go farther. Isn't that really the goal for our lives? We're invited to "run with endurance the race God has set before us" (Heb. 12:1). Not run with speed but with *endurance*. Rhythms help us go the distance.

If you've been pushing yourself hard as an introvert, you have permission to slow down. If you've been trying to keep up with the hurried pace of the world around you, you're allowed to stop hustling. If you're worn out and weary from trying so hard all the time, you're invited by Jesus to

"learn the unforced *rhythms of grace*" (MATT. 11:28–30 MSG).

IN THIS MOMENT

We can have rhythms in every area of our lives. Use this space to brain-storm introvert-friendly ideas. But note: if something makes you feel guilty or like it's a "have to," then cross it out.

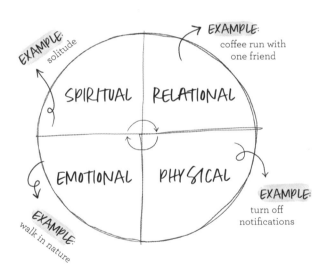

There is an ebb and flow to life. Rhythms are in everything we do. There are times to push hard and times to rest and recuperate.

—GREG MCKEOWN

yesterday

A moment that filled me up was . . .

A moment that drained me was . . .

TA—DA! LIST

1. _____

_____

2. _____

_____

3. _____

_____

today

One thing I'm worried about today is . . .

One thing I'm grateful for today is . . .

MY "DO WHAT YOU CAN" PLAN

1. _____

_____

2. _____

_____

3. _____

_____

thoughts, feelings, ALL THE THINGS

six

remember you're not the only one

One of the most common phrases I hear when I connect with introverts is "I thought I was the only one." I thought I was the only one who sometimes dreads spending time with people, even if I love them.

I thought I was the only one who wishes the world would turn the volume down for a while, especially on social media.

I thought I was the only one who occasionally goes blank in the middle of conversations at the worst possible times.

I thought I was the only one who would pick a quiet walk in nature or a deep conversation over a party or other activities I'm told are "fun."

I thought I was the only one who _____.

After engaging with thousands of introverts, I can say with confidence, "You're not the only one." While we perceive the world around us as extroverted, when the Myers & Briggs Foundation looked at thirty years of test results from sources such as the Stanford Research Institute, they found that 50.7 percent of people are introverts.[1] (Interestingly, a recent global leadership sample put the percentage slightly higher at 56.8 percent.[2]) In any given room, half of those around you are also likely thinking of hiding in the bathroom, wondering when they can go home, or feeling awkward.

In an interview, actress Emma Watson said, "I'm . . . an introverted kind of person just by nature, it's not like a conscious choice that I'm making necessarily. It's genuinely who I am. . . . If you're anything other than an extravert you're made to think there's something wrong with you. That's like the story of my life. Coming to realize that about myself was very empowering."[3]

I believe God intentionally made half the world introverts. He's strategically positioned us in every area of life—business, nonprofit organizations, schools, hospitals, churches, neighborhoods, families. It's tempting to change who we are in order to fit into these places. But what our introvert hearts really long for isn't conformity; it's true connection. It's the feeling of being known and loved as we are. That can happen only when we have the courage to be who God made us. When

10 FAMOUS PEOPLE YOU MIGHT NOT KNOW ARE INTROVERTS

Oprah Winfrey	Abraham Lincoln	Max Lucado
C. S. Lewis	Albert Einstein	Jerry Seinfeld
Michael Jordan	Rosa Parks	
Bill Gates	Joanna Gaines	

we give ourselves permission to be who we are, we also make others feel less alone—especially our fellow introverts.

> "We are many parts of *one body*, and we all belong to *each other*" (ROM. 12:5).

You are not the only one when it comes to your struggles. But you are the only one when it comes to your gifts, purpose, and God's plan for you. You're the only one who can offer what he's placed within you, love people in your unique way, and display his image to the world in exactly the way you do.

You're never the only one, but you're always irreplaceable.

IN THIS MOMENT

Who are some of your favorite introverts? What do you love or admire about them?

_____

_____

_____

_____

_____

_____

_____

_____

I'm an introvert.... I love being by myself, love being outdoors, love taking a long walk with my dogs and looking at the trees, flowers, and the sky.

—AUDREY HEPBURN

yesterday

A moment that filled me up was . . .

A moment that drained me was . . .

TA—DA! LIST

1. _____

_____

2. _____

_____

3. _____

_____

today

One thing I'm worried about today is . . .

One thing I'm grateful for today is . . .

MY "DO WHAT YOU CAN" PLAN

1. _____

_____

2. _____

_____

3. _____

_____

thoughts, feelings, ALL THE THINGS

seven

see struggles as the other end of strengths

In elementary school, I made frequent visits to the nurse's office. "I have a stomachache," I'd say. The kind nurse, perhaps knowing what was really going on, would escort me to a mercifully quiet room with a little blue cot, where she'd let me lie down for a few minutes until I was ready to return to class.

Looking back, a chaotic elementary school classroom was simply too much for my little introvert nervous system to handle at times. That same nervous system made me an empathetic, considerate, and creative kid—it was a source of many strengths, not just occasional stomachaches.

> **What signs can you see in your childhood that indicated you were an introvert (example: needing quiet, listening well to your friends, loving to read)?**

The nurse seemed to know this and honored all of who I was, but it would be several more decades before I learned to do the same. Embracing who we truly are takes courage and hard work, especially if we've felt pressure to be someone we're not. My counseling and life-coaching clients, especially introverts, often show up like I did at the nurse's office and say, "There's a part of myself I don't want. Help me get rid of it."

Even the apostle Paul begged God several times to take away something he saw as a weakness. The divine answer he received?

"My *grace* is all you need. My power works best in *weakness*" (2 COR. 12:9).

Over the years I, like Paul, have come to believe what's most powerful is not elimination but transformation. Who we are comes with potential struggles and strengths. That's true for all of us, whether we're extroverts or introverts.

For example, because of their highly reactive nervous systems, introverts are more likely to struggle with anxiety.[1] However, those same nervous systems also mean introverts often have a strong sense of empathy.

What if a struggle is just the other end of a strength?

STRUGGLE ———————————————— STRENGTH

Anxiety   **Empathy**

Growth happens not by changing who we are but by learning how to move away from struggles and toward our strengths. Doing so activates our gifts, increases our well-being, and empowers us to make our greatest contributions to the world. This realization has changed my life, and I believe it will change yours.

We live in a noisy, chaotic culture. We're all looking for less stress and more peace, less noise and more meaning, less hurry and more rest. I believe introverts can lead the way, and we can all move toward a stronger life today.

Growth HAPPENS NOT BY CHANGING WHO WE ARE BUT BY LEARNING HOW TO MOVE AWAY FROM struggles AND TOWARD OUR strengths.

IN THIS MOMENT

BREATH PRAYER:

*God, lead me away from my struggles
and toward my strengths one small,
grace-filled step at a time.*

What's one of your struggles? What's one of your strengths?

Struggle _____

Strength _____

So you're quiet and you don't always know what to say? On the other side of that "weakness" is a powerful, analytical mind. You get overstimulated more easily than others? In your solitude, you solve problems, think of new ideas, and create. You "umm" and "ahh" when you speak? Your reflective mind processes things deeply. Instead of seeing your introvert qualities as your biggest flaws, consider that they may actually be your biggest strengths.

—JENN GRANNEMAN

yesterday

A moment that filled me up was . . .

A moment that drained me was . . .

TA–DA! LIST

1. _____

_____

2. _____

_____

3. _____

_____

today

One thing I'm worried about today is . . .

One thing I'm grateful for today is . . .

MY "DO WHAT YOU CAN" PLAN

1. _____

_____

2. _____

_____

3. _____

_____

thoughts, feelings, ALL THE THINGS

eight

choose quality over quantity

God doesn't tell us how much time we're to spend with others, how many friendships we should maintain, or which social activities we must do. Instead, he describes love this way:

Love is *patient* and *kind.* Love is not jealous or boastful or proud or rude. It does not demand its own way. It is not irritable, and it keeps no record of being wronged. It does not rejoice about injustice but *rejoices* whenever the truth wins out. Love never gives up, never loses *faith,* is always *hopeful,* and *endures* through every circumstance.[1]

None of us live this list perfectly. What I want us to focus on today is the idea that being a loving person is not about popularity but rather *purposeful relationships*. It's about how we treat each person in our path. When an expert in the law asked Jesus what it meant to love your neighbor, he replied with the parable of the good Samaritan, a simple story about one person helping another.

I sometimes picture a system that operates on the principle of more people in my life = I'm a more loving person.

I'm a more loving person if . . .

Is what you wrote *really* true? If not, what is?

I've heard other introverts express something similar. But love isn't about the number of people we have in our lives or likes we get online or guests who come to our wedding (or funeral) or contacts in our phone. Our social schedules aren't a measuring stick for our spirituality. If we want to grow in love, we must measure nothing. Instead, make one connection, have one conversation, show kindness to one person at a time—which introverts naturally do well.

When I encounter introverts who feel isolated, they often share the same root cause: pretending to be extroverts. Yes, acting like an extrovert means putting yourself out there more, spending an increased amount of time with people, even making small talk. It might even make you feel more popular. But it's lonely to feel like you can't be yourself, no matter how many people are in the room.

Bestselling author and researcher Brené Brown says,

> Belonging is the innate human desire to be part of something larger than us. Because this yearning is so primal, we often try to acquire it by fitting in and by seeking approval, which are not only hollow substitutes for belonging, but often barriers to it. Because true belonging only happens when we present our authentic, imperfect selves to the world, our sense of belonging can never be greater than our level of self-acceptance.[2]

How would you describe what true belonging means to you? True belonging is . . .

I believe what introverts need most is not a skill set but a shift in mindset. It's the courage to decide that who God created us to be is enough. It's the bravery to see that for us, "loving well" looks different. It's the bold step of showing up as we are, with vulnerability and without apology. As I write in *Fiercehearted*,

Jesus said we all must **deny ourselves,** and perhaps this is part of what he meant. That at some point in our lives, WE MUST GIVE UP TRYING TO BECOME SOMEONE HE NEVER INTENDED US TO BE.[3]

IN THIS MOMENT

BREATH PRAYER:
God, you have called me to a life of purposeful relationships instead of the pressure of popularity.

Who has God placed in your life for you to love? Write down a few names that come to mind.

_____

_____

_____

_____

_____

_____

_____

_____

_____

_____

Bravely following Jesus means accepting and loving who I am, because it's who he created me to be.

—ALIZA LATTA

yesterday

today

A moment that filled me up was . . .

One thing I'm worried about today is . . .

A moment that drained me was . . .

One thing I'm grateful for today is . . .

TA—DA! LIST

MY "DO WHAT YOU CAN" PLAN

1.

1.

2.

2.

3.

3.

thoughts, feelings, ALL THE THINGS

nine

never settle
for self-esteem

I'm part of a panel at a women's event, and those of us on stage are asked, "Do you ever struggle with confidence? It looks like all of you have it together." I've been asked this before, told this before, and it still surprises and startles me. Because I can see my insides. I know my messes and my crazy, my mistakes and my stumbles, how I've wrestled with depression and anxiety like wild alligators, how my heart has the scars to prove it.

The woman who gets the microphone first is lovely and confident, outgoing and articulate. By the time it's my turn, my heart is pounding, I'm sweating, and I feel like I have something in my nose (which always happens when I'm speaking in public). I tell the audience all this and they laugh with me, thankfully.

Then I also say what God has been putting on my heart, what has been saving me from myself, what has been making me stronger and bolder in ways that have been catching me by surprise. I declare to this group of women and to my imperfect self, "What I've been realizing lately is this: *the world tells us we need to have self-esteem, but what we really need is holy confidence."*

Self-esteem is . . .

Holy confidence is . . .

I've especially needed to learn this as an introvert. I battled self-doubt over my ability to make small talk or feel comfortable in groups. But slowly God began to show me I'm created as an introvert, that what I saw as flaws were actually strengths. I listened well, had deep empathy, knew how to champion one person at a time. As we've talked about, research also now shows that we're created as introverts and extroverts with differences in our brains and nervous systems.

Before I spent years studying what it meant to be an introvert, before I became comfortable in my God-given skin, I tried to prove I was enough. Perfect enough. Good enough. Experienced enough. Smart enough. Pretty enough. But it's only when we come to the place where we can finally say "I'm not enough, but Jesus is" that our hearts get free.

I'M NOT *enough,* BUT JESUS IS.

I feel like I need to be . . .

_____ enough

_____ enough

_____ enough

The reality is, despite our strengths and being wonderfully made, we will still sometimes fall short of the expectations of others and ourselves. But it doesn't matter because our scandalous God, our gracious Savior, declares that we are beloved and chosen and empowered *anyway*.

"My heart is *confident* in you, O God" (PS. 57:7).

Self-esteem says we can do it.

Holy confidence says, despite us, God will.

In the moments when I'm still insecure and afraid, when my heart is pounding, my hands are sweating, and it feels like there's something in my nose, that's the truth I really need to know. Maybe, just maybe, I'm not the only one.

IN THIS MOMENT

God, you are the source of my confidence and true identity. You're the one who tells me who I am.

Who is someone you think has it all together? Pause for a moment and pray for that person, who likely has more struggles and insecurities than you can see.

_____

_____

_____

_____

_____

_____

_____

_____

_____

You don't have to hold it all together. You are held by grace.

—KAITLYN BOUCHILLON

yesterday

A moment that filled me up was . . .

A moment that drained me was . . .

TA—DA! LIST

1. _____

2. _____

3. _____

today

One thing I'm worried about today is . . .

One thing I'm grateful for today is . . .

MY "DO WHAT YOU CAN" PLAN

1. _____

2. _____

3. _____

thoughts, feelings, ALL THE THINGS

ten

dare to show up
as you are

Imagine you're an eavesdropper in the garden of Eden on the day Adam and Eve eat the forbidden fruit.

The man and his wife heard the LORD God walking about in the garden. SO THEY HID FROM THE LORD GOD AMONG THE TREES. Then the LORD God called to the man, "Where are you?"

He replied, "I heard you walking in the garden, so I hid. I was afraid because I was naked."

"WHO TOLD YOU THAT YOU WERE NAKED?" the LORD God asked. "Have you eaten from the tree whose fruit I commanded you not to eat?"[1]

We've seen this story depicted in beautiful artwork. But let's get real, it's like going to Sunday school and forgetting your pants, except worse—much worse. What do Adam and Eve do about their feelings of awkwardness? They hide. And humanity has been doing the same ever since.

What sometimes makes you want to hide? What gives you courage?

We hide because we're imperfect, vulnerable, and afraid. Even if we don't jump behind a bush, we learn how to cover up our feelings, desires, and true selves.

Hiding isn't the same as taking time alone as an introvert. How can you tell the difference? Hiding comes from *shame*. We feel inadequate. We're afraid of rejection. We're drained by self-doubt and disconnected from God and those around us. We all hide. We all want to be found.

So we post the perfect pictures on Instagram. Work the crowd. Craft an image. Create an audience instead of relationships. Avoid all the awkward.

But despite its difficulties, I'm falling in love with the awkward. It's where we find out which one of our friends laughs so hard, he snorts. Where we discover how beautiful the ugly cry can be. Remember we're not God—and that's a good thing. It's where we learn to believe we're loved for who we are, not who we sometimes wish we could become.

What do you love about the awkward, imperfect people in your life?

The people who impress me most aren't the ones on stages or with the most likes. I'm impressed by those who show up and say, "Here I am. There you are. Let's figure out how to love each other." That's a brave, fierce, world-changing thing.

I'm often asked, "How do I connect with people?" But the real question being asked is "How do I connect in a risk-free, rejection-protected, non-awkward way?" The gut-honest answer: you don't. There's no avoiding the disappointment, fear, and inconvenience of true connection.

So let's extend the invitation, send the text, start the conversation. Community isn't something we find; it's something we create one person at a time. As introverts, we love well in ways that are needed more than ever before.

Insecurity might point out our imperfections, but grace invites us to come as we are. Shame might tell us to try harder, but our worth is an unearned gift. Fear might tempt us to hide, but it's not too late to show up.

Community isn't something we find; it's something we create one person at a time.

IN THIS MOMENT

God, give me the courage to simply show up
today and trust you will take care of the rest.

Picture an awkward moment with someone else that turned out to be
a moment of unexpected connection or became a funny story you love
to tell. Record it below.

_____

_____

_____

_____

_____

_____

_____

_____

_____

We are talented, deeply committed people who are vital beings in a
world that needs kindness, creative thought, quiet reflection, caring,
and listening.

—KIM CRABBE

yesterday

A moment that filled me up was . . .

A moment that drained me was . . .

1. _____

   _____

2. _____

   _____

3. _____

   _____

today

One thing I'm worried about today is . . .

One thing I'm grateful for today is . . .

MY "DO WHAT YOU CAN" PLAN

1. _____

   _____

2. _____

   _____

3. _____

   _____

thoughts, feelings, ALL THE THINGS

eleven

know your influence matters

True influence isn't about getting attention; it's about making a connection. Daniel Goleman says in *Social Intelligence*, "Even our most routine encounters act as regulators in the brain, priming our emotions, some desirable, others not. The more strongly connected we are with someone emotionally, the greater the mutual force."[1]

Think of *the* most influential people in your life. Your answers are likely "Mom" or "my teacher" rather than "Nobel Prize winner" or "CEO." Yes, those in the public eye get more attention, but attention isn't the same as meaningful influence. Caring matters more than charisma.

Who has influenced you most?

Pastor Brandon Cox says, "Be you. Be the leader God carefully crafted from the womb. Know your strengths and weaknesses. Intentionally grow in areas you find challenging as a leader. But reject the pressure to conform to a certain image of what a good leader must look like."[2] His leadership theory? The "absolute, very best personality type to possess" is *yours*.[3]

Jesus, the ultimate example of influence, focused most of his time on twelve people, traveled less than two hundred miles from his birthplace, lived to thirty-three (and spent thirty of those years in obscurity), and died as a rebel on a cross in the name of love. Yet after he came, nothing was ever the same.

We still need men and women who choose a different kind of influence. Who refuse to shine the spotlight on themselves and instead turn it toward others. Our fame-loving culture needs people brave enough to walk off the stage to talk with one person in the crowd. Companies and communities need leaders who are not glory chasers but gracious servants of others.

"You are the *light* of the world" (MATT. 5:14).

What's a small thing someone did that made a big difference to you?

So, let's kiss our babies or close the big sale. Get on a plane or walk to the local park. Clear our throats and say what we're afraid to or offer the gift of silence to a world in desperate need of it. Raise our hands to volunteer or say the brave no our souls long to hear. Make wedding cakes or millions of dollars for a good cause. Go with a friend to chemotherapy or be the keynote speaker at a conference.

But let's never believe our quiet nature disqualifies us from changing the world.

We may find it's the very thing that empowers us to do so.

IN THIS MOMENT

God, use me as I am, where I am,
with whatever I have today.

Think of one person who has touched your life and might not know it
(or could use a reminder). Send them a text or note to let them know.
You can write their name and what you'd like to tell them below.

_____

_____

_____

_____

_____

_____

If you are an introvert, chances are that you've tried to influence others
by mirroring your more outgoing colleagues. My guess is that such an
approach isn't working for you: it's exhausting, unsustainable, and ul-
timately ineffective. Contrary to what most books on influence will tell
you, the answer isn't about becoming the extrovert you aren't. I believe,
however, that you will become a more effective influencer when you stop
trying to act like an extrovert and instead make the most of your natural,
quiet strengths.

—JENNIFER KAHNWEILER

yesterday

A moment that filled me up was . . .

A moment that drained me was . . .

TA—DA! LIST

1.

2.

3.

today

One thing I'm worried about today is . . .

One thing I'm grateful for today is . . .

MY "DO WHAT YOU CAN" PLAN

1.

2.

3.

thoughts, feelings, ALL THE THINGS

twelve

believe you can handle it

"I can't do this."

When do you say this to yourself? Maybe it's when you walk into a crowded room. It might be at church when signing up for a small group unexpectedly triggers big fears. Perhaps it's when you want to offer your idea in a meeting at work but stare at your notepad instead. It's even more likely in serious situations—when you need to talk to a doctor about a diagnosis, when avoiding conflict starts pushing your relationship to a breaking point, when presenting a project at work means the difference between getting a raise and sending out your résumé.

When have you felt like saying, "I can't do this"?

I've said "I can't do this" to myself thousands of times, in various situations, but they all seem to have this in common: they push me outside my comfort zone. It makes sense that we would feel this way, because as introverts, we do need to be aware of our limits in a chaotic, overwhelming world. This discernment empowers us to be intentional about how we use our energy and where we direct our emotions. But sometimes what's helpful becomes a trap that holds us back.

Just this morning I pictured a goal for my future and instantly heard that phrase again: "I can't do this." But this time I paused and asked, "Why not?" I have the God who spoke the universe into being dwelling within me. He created me for a specific purpose and has promised to provide all I need. I am loved, worthy, and capable. I prayed, "God, free me from self-imposed limits."

Dr. Susan Jeffers, author of *Feel the Fear and Do It Anyway*, says,

> At the bottom of every one of your fears is simply the fear that you can't handle WHATEVER life may bring you.[1]

I'd modify that slightly for us and say, "At the bottom of every one of your fears *as an introvert* is simply the fear that you can't handle whatever life may bring you."

We tell ourselves things like . . .
I can't handle SMALL TALK.
I can't handle CONFLICT.

I can't handle REJECTION.

I can't handle _____.

I can't handle _____.

I can't handle _____.

But the reality is, *we can*. Paul said,

"I have learned the secret of living in every situation. . . .
I can do everything *through Christ,*
who gives me strength" (PHIL. 4:12–13).

This doesn't mean everything will be easy, comfortable, or come naturally to us as introverts. It also doesn't mean we should try to do everything; we still need to use wisdom in choosing God's best for us. But it does mean we don't have to live with self-imposed limits anymore.

Instead of saying, "Because I'm an introvert, I can't do this," we can learn to say, "Yes, this will be uncomfortable and challenging, but with Jesus I can handle anything today."

IN THIS MOMENT

BREATH PRAYER:
*God, you empower me to do all
things through your strength.*

Imagine a moment when you told yourself "I can't do this," then you did it anyway. What did you learn from that experience that you can remember today?

_____

_____

_____

_____

_____

_____

_____

_____

_____

I was an introvert with asthma. And now? I'm still an introvert with asthma, but now I can deadlift 225 pounds, do judo throws, hip thrust 400 pounds, and knock out 10 pullups in a row.

—BRIE LARSON, star of Marvel's first female superhero movie

yesterday

A moment that filled me up was . . .

A moment that drained me was . . .

TA—DA! LIST

1. _____

2. _____

3. _____

today

One thing I'm worried about today is . . .

One thing I'm grateful for today is . . .

MY "DO WHAT YOU CAN" PLAN

1. _____

2. _____

3. _____

thoughts, feelings, ALL THE THINGS

thirteen

pursue the goal of a quiet life

Mark and I have a small sign in our home office that reads, "Make it your goal to live a quiet life" (1 Thess. 4:11). I often think of how differently modern culture would write this statement:

Make it your goal to live a loud life.

Make it your goal to live a big life.

Make it your goal to live a famous life.

Make it your goal to live a _____ life.

It's deeply reassuring to Mark and me, as introverts, that instead we're invited to live a *quiet* life. Why does it seem there's so much opposition to doing so?

In the book *Meditation for Fidgety Skeptics*, author and journalist Dan Harris meets with various people to talk about what keeps them from taking time for solitude and reflection. Some of the reasons he heard included that being alone felt vulnerable, uncomfortable, or even fear provoking.

What do you think makes being quiet hard for so many people?

I once sat in a course where the instructor asked us to be silent for a minute to prove doing so wasn't easy. As an introvert, I found this exercise interesting, because being quiet is easy for me. I find silence much simpler and more manageable than making small talk at a dinner party.

I mention all this because I hear from fellow introverts who feel guilty for having or wanting a quiet life. But I had this aha moment: many people choose a loud life because quiet requires the courage to confront their own thoughts, hearts, and souls. In other words, a quiet life is often not one of retreating but one of *great courage*.

It's in the quiet that we more clearly hear the whisper of God.

It's in the quiet that we create, innovate, dream, plan.

It's in the quiet that we realign with our truest selves.

It's in the quiet that we have room to think about how to serve others.

It's in the quiet that our inner wells are filled so we have more to pour out.

It's in the quiet that we _____.

Certain seasons or situations can make actual *physical* quiet almost impossible. For example, we might be chasing toddlers or in the middle of a big work project or in social justice conversations that call for speaking up. In those cases, the goal can be learning to (slowly, imperfectly) cultivate quiet on the *inside* when we're surrounded by noise.

Even in seasons and situations like these, a rhythm of quiet solitude can be helpful. That may mean scheduling quiet as if it were an important meeting, sitting in our car for five minutes, or the introvert classic—briefly hiding in the bathroom.

Quiet moments aren't selfish. Instead, they're essential for a lifetime of loving and serving well.

So let's never underestimate the power of a quiet life—one that doesn't make headlines or get a million likes, looks ordinary on the surface, isn't trendy or the next hot topic. If you, as a fellow introvert, have ever felt guilty for loving or pursuing quiet, then it's time for a change in perspective.

Quiet MOMENTS AREN'T SELFISH. INSTEAD, THEY'RE *essential* FOR A LIFETIME OF LOVING AND SERVING WELL.

A quiet life is brave.

A quiet life is intentional.

A quiet life is revolutionary.

A quiet life is about value, not volume.

A quiet life is a worthy, even holy, goal.

A quiet life is _____.

IN THIS MOMENT

BREATH PRAYER:
*God, today I choose to see
the gifts in quietness.*

Spend ten minutes in quiet today. Notice what makes it hard and what's helpful to you. You can use the space below to record your observations.

_____

_____

_____

_____

_____

_____

_____

_____

My life is marked now by quiet, connection, simplicity. . . . There is a peace that defines my days, a settledness, a groundedness. I've been searching for this in a million places, all outside myself, and it astounds me to realize that the groundedness is within me, and that maybe it was there all along. Now I know that the best thing I can offer to this world is not my force or energy, but a well-tended spirit, a wise and brave soul.

—SHAUNA NIEQUIST

yesterday

A moment that filled me up was . . .

A moment that drained me was . . .

TA—DA! LIST

1. _____

2. _____

3. _____

today

One thing I'm worried about today is . . .

One thing I'm grateful for today is . . .

MY "DO WHAT YOU CAN" PLAN

1. _____

2. _____

3. _____

thoughts, feelings, ALL THE THINGS

fourteen
overcome overthinking

The city where I live placed a traffic circle close to my house. For weeks I tried to avoid it. But I finally became tired of taking back roads and determined to master this new phenomenon. I discovered if you don't know how to exit it, a traffic circle becomes your personal merry-go-round, much to the dismay of other drivers. Sometimes our active introvert minds can feel like a traffic circle, and we get into endless loops of thinking without resolution.

The kind of thinking I'm describing here is overthinking, a fancy name for worry. It focuses on our circumstances—what happened in the past, what's going on now, or what might occur in the future. Emotions such as sadness, anger, frustration, or regret are healthy parts of the human experience. Only when we get stuck in those emotions and thoughts do we impact our mental and physical health.

What do you tend to worry about or overthink?

The good news is, there are ways you can exit overthinking—and you can learn them, just as I eventually learned to navigate that pesky traffic circle.

4 Ways to Get Your Mind Unstuck

1. TELL GOD AND/OR SOMEONE ELSE. Rumination happens in isolation. Letting someone else into our mind loop can break the cycle. "Let the Spirit renew your thoughts and attitudes" (Eph. 4:23).

2. DISTRACT YOURSELF. We can learn from the extroverts in our lives. They're often masters at getting their minds off unpleasant things by engaging in fun or meaningful activities.

3. THINK OF THREE OTHER EXPLANATIONS. We tend to forget that our perceptions are only one explanation for events. When we force ourselves to come up with alternate stories, we weaken rumination.

4. TAKE ONE SMALL STEP. When we overthink, we're unable to move forward. To get out of analysis paralysis, think of one small step. Bonus points if it's doable in five minutes or less.

Introverts are more vulnerable to overthinking because of our highly active minds. So many of the strengths introverts have, like our capacity for reflection, deep understanding of others, and creative imaginations, come from the same active brains that also cause us to overthink. When you find yourself stuck in overthinking, don't be hard on yourself. Instead, remind yourself that though this tendency needs to be managed, it is also tied to some extraordinary parts of who you are.

The traffic circle annoys me at times, but it also helps me get where I want to go. Our introvert minds are often the same way. As author and introvert advocate Jenn Granneman says, "Introverts, you have powerful minds. Overthinking, when used the right way, can be one of your greatest assets."[1]

"INTROVERTS,
YOU HAVE POWERFUL MINDS.
Overthinking,
WHEN USED THE RIGHT WAY,
CAN BE ONE OF YOUR
GREATEST ASSETS."

IN THIS MOMENT

BREATH PRAYER:
God, you've given me a remarkable mind,
and I will focus it on what moves
me forward with you today.

Try one of the strategies from the 4 Ways to Get Your Mind Unstuck list today. You can write down which one you picked and how it worked for you below.

Research on the brain has found that introverts experience even more internal chatter than extroverts.... Be aware of the messages you say to yourself and how they affect you. If you don't like them, change them. Remind yourself to do so every day. Speak to yourself—privately and publicly—the way you'd speak to your best friend: with respect and kindness.

—NANCY ANCOWITZ

yesterday

A moment that filled me up was ...

A moment that drained me was ...

today

One thing I'm worried about today is ...

One thing I'm grateful for today is ...

TA—DA! LIST

1. _____
   _____
2. _____
   _____
3. _____
   _____

MY "DO WHAT YOU CAN" PLAN

1. _____
   _____
2. _____
   _____
3. _____
   _____

thoughts, feelings, ALL THE THINGS

fifteen

understand why you're not shy

"Don't be shy" is a command almost every introvert child has heard at some point. It might come from a well-meaning parent, teacher, or other adult who mistakenly thinks quietness is something to be conquered rather than encouraged.

If that happened to you, *I'm so sorry*. The labels placed on us in childhood can stick to our hearts long after we're grown up. We carry them around with a vague sense of shame, as if there might be something wrong with us that we still haven't figured out how to fix.

But I want to rip that label off today because being an introvert doesn't mean you're shy. Since introversion is such a big part of who we are, it matters that we also understand what it is *not*. Susan Cain, author of *Quiet*, says, "Shyness is the fear of negative judgment, and introversion is a preference for quiet, minimally stimulating environments."[1]

In Your Own Words

Shyness is . . .

Being an introvert is . . .

Yes, as an introvert you may sometimes *feel* shy, but so does the rest of humanity. That doesn't mean shy is your identity. Ninety percent of people describe themselves as shy at some point during their lives. Thirteen percent will be diagnosed with social anxiety.[2] Shyness and social anxiety are about fear; introversion is about how we're wired. An extrovert skipping a party because she's afraid of not fitting in feels shy; an introvert choosing a book as her Friday night companion feels content.

A question we can ask ourselves as introverts is, "Am I living out of fear right now?" If the answer is yes (and it will be for all of us at times), we can pause and return to our true identity.

"The Spirit God gave us does not make us timid, but gives us power, love and self-discipline" (2 Tim. 1:7 NIV). This verse is sometimes distorted to imply that we need to be more extroverted. But sometimes staying quiet is the most powerful choice.

Sometimes love looks like listening. Sometimes self-discipline means faithfully serving behind the scenes.

Today we can say, "God intentionally created me. He has a plan and a purpose for my life. I'm his beloved child, and he has promised to provide everything I need for all he has called me to do. I'm not listening to old lies or false limitations. I will take the next step of obedience with courage, trusting that with God, anything is possible. I'm not shy; I'm a divinely designed introvert who is here for such a time as this."

IN THIS MOMENT

What's a label that has been placed on you as an introvert? Write it below, cross through it, and write new words that reflect the truth about who you are (example: shy/created as an introvert).

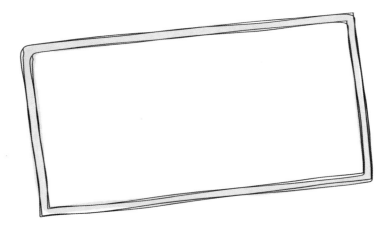

Shy and introverted; two words that are often used interchangeably, in fact, they are regularly considered to have identical meanings. In reality, they are quite different. While one stems from a lack of confidence in oneself, the other stems from a preference for a quiet environment. One is something that can be improved through self-reflection and personal growth, the other a way of being and operating in the world.

—WHITNEY BARKMAN

yesterday

A moment that filled me up was . . .

A moment that drained me was . . .

today

One thing I'm worried about today is . . .

One thing I'm grateful for today is . . .

TA—DA! LIST

1.

2.

3.

MY "DO WHAT YOU CAN" PLAN

1.

2.

3.

thoughts, feelings, ALL THE THINGS

sixteen

get a new perspective on joy

"Smile!" my family member says at a holiday get-together, slapping me on the back as if that will force some exuberance out of me. I'm startled, and the expression I make is definitely *not* a smile. I'd been contentedly observing from the sidelines, taking a moment to catch my breath amid all the chaos that often comes with this time of year.

Along with "don't be shy" and "you're so quiet," the exhortation to "smile!" has followed me throughout my life as an introvert. At times this has even made me question myself. *Am I not a happy person?* Or in spiritual settings, *Do I not have joy?*

INTROVERTS AND EXTROVERTS EXPERIENCE AND EXPRESS *happiness* DIFFERENTLY.

One of the biggest aha moments I had while writing *The Powerful Purpose of Introverts* was that introverts and extroverts experience and express happiness differently. Because of the extrovert preference for the neurotransmitter dopamine, their style of happiness and joy is

YOUR HAPPINESS SYNONYMS

All the words below can be emotional synonyms for *happy*. Highlight or circle at least three that resonate with you.

For me, feeling happy = feeling . . .

Affectionate	Empowered	Interested	Strong
Altruistic	Energized	Motivated	Surprised
Amused	Engaged	Optimistic	Worshipful
Awed	Enthusiastic	Passionate	Add your own:
Blissful	Excited	Peaceful	
Calm	Fascinated	Productive	_____
Cheerful	Focused	Purposeful	
Confident	Free	Relaxed	_____
Content	Fulfilled	Satisfied	
Delighted	Grateful	Secure	_____
Eager	Inspired	Serene	
			_____

enthusiasm and excitement. Because of the introvert preference for acetylcholine, happiness and joy are related more to calm and contentment. So which type is right? *Both.*

When we talk about happiness, what we're often trying to describe is something much deeper. *Shalom* is a word that has no equivalent in our language. It's often translated as "happiness," "joy," or "peace," but none of these words capture its full meaning. Shalom appears over two hundred times in Scripture, for example in Psalm 35:27: "The LORD . . .

delights in the well-being of his servant" (NIV). Theologian and author Tim Keller says,

> SHALOM experienced is multidimensional, complete well-being—physical, psychological, social, and spiritual; it flows from all of one's relationships being put right—with God, with(in) oneself, and with others.[1]

As I stood at the edge of that holiday gathering, I felt *shalom*, a sense of belonging, gratitude, and satisfaction. My family member seemed to be experiencing it too. I watched him tell yet another story to a group of people seated around the table who appreciatively laughed out loud.

Introvert, there is nothing wrong with you if you aren't as outwardly giddy as others. It's okay if your version of happiness is peaceful and reflective. You are just as spiritual if joy is a quiet hum within your heart rather than an enthusiastic cheer. Because our extroverts love us, we may need to explain what happiness and joy look and feel like in our worlds. They worry about us sometimes, and most of us have experienced the kindhearted awkwardness of an extrovert trying to cheer us up when we're perfectly fine already.

My family member's intentions with me were good, just misguided. He didn't realize that sometimes we smile with our faces, but often, and even more importantly, we do so with our souls.

IN THIS MOMENT

BREATH PRAYER:
*God, you are my Shalom, the source
and sustainer of all true happiness and joy.*

Close your eyes and picture a moment when you experienced *shalom*, a sense of true well-being. What are you thankful for when you reflect on it?

_____

_____

_____

_____

_____

_____

_____

_____

I used to believe the search for happiness was a superficial pursuit, that happiness and holiness were mutually exclusive. But now I understand they go hand in hand. This work of seeking authentic happiness is important, and it is holy.

—ALLI WORTHINGTON

yesterday

A moment that filled me up was . . .

A moment that drained me was . . .

TA—DA! LIST

1. _____

_____

2. _____

_____

3. _____

_____

today

One thing I'm worried about today is . . .

One thing I'm grateful for today is . . .

MY "DO WHAT YOU CAN" PLAN

1. _____

_____

2. _____

_____

3. _____

_____

thoughts, feelings, ALL THE THINGS

seventeen

honor your need for rest

"You just need to get some rest" is something well-meaning people may say to us introverts if they know us well enough to recognize when we're depleted. So we manage to sleep in on a Saturday or sit on the couch catching up on our favorite show for a few hours, then wonder why we still feel drained. Our culture tells us rest is simply a lack of activity.

But what if there's more to it? Dr. Saundra Dalton-Smith studies rest, and she's found there are seven different types we need. Instead of a single solution, like sleep, we need a variety of strategies for being restored (especially as introverts).

7 Kinds of Rest

1. PHYSICAL. Yes, we do need to give our bodies a break. Dalton-Smith explains we can rest our body in passive ways, like a nap, or in active ones, like a walk outside on a beautiful day.

2. MENTAL. Our introvert brains work hard for us, whether we're completing a project or pondering a problem. We need to give them time off, like when we zone out, daydream, meditate, or just watch the birds in our backyard.

3. SENSORY. Introverts have especially sensitive nervous systems, which means sometimes we need time away from sounds, light, noise, and everything else we take in through our senses.

4. CREATIVE. Even as adults, we need time to play without forcing ourselves to be productive. We can work a puzzle, read fiction, or make muffins—whatever we like to do just for the joy of it.

5. EMOTIONAL. We need to give ourselves permission to do things like say no more often, take a break from social media, or surround ourselves with positive people.

6. SOCIAL. Solitude is essential for the long-term well-being of introverts. Making space for it in our lives isn't selfish; it equips us for a life of service.

7. SPIRITUAL. From the very beginning of creation, God included rest. He doesn't measure our spirituality by how much we can do. What he wants is an **intimate relationship** with us.[1]

Dr. Dalton-Smith says,

> The ultimate purpose of sacred rest is for you to enjoy God, enjoy people, and enjoy your life's splendor. Sacred rest is worth the journey into your best life. It is a chance for your faith to be strengthened as you learn how to lean on Him and how to accomplish more even when physically doing less. It's becoming reacquainted with the life you've created and how you can enjoy it to the fullest.[2]

"The LORD is my *Shepherd*;
I have all that I need.
He lets me rest in green meadows;
he leads me beside peaceful streams.
He *renews* my strength" (PS. 23:1–3).

Rest isn't a guilty pleasure; it's a grace-filled gift from a God who wants us to thrive. It isn't a sign we're struggling; in our always-busy culture, it's a show of true strength. It's not laziness but a way we can love ourselves, others, and God. What if instead of viewing our need for rest as a weakness, we see it as an opportunity to model a healthier, holier way of living within an exhausted world?

IN THIS MOMENT

BREATH PRAYER:
God, you freely offer the gift of rest to me.
Help me embrace it with joy
and gratitude, not guilt or resistance.

Write down an idea for each of the 7 types of rest (example: physical rest = nap).

1. Physical rest:

2. Mental rest:

3. Sensory rest:

4. Creative rest:

5. Emotional rest:

6. Social rest:

7. Spiritual rest:

When we follow the Savior, we can be assured that in God's yes, there will always be an element of rest.

—SUSIE LARSON

yesterday

A moment that filled me up was . . .

A moment that drained me was . . .

1. _____

_____

2. _____

_____

3. _____

_____

today

One thing I'm worried about today is . . .

One thing I'm grateful for today is . . .

MY "DO WHAT YOU CAN" PLAN

1. _____

_____

2. _____

_____

3. _____

_____

thoughts, feelings, ALL THE THINGS

eighteen

let nature speak to your soul

"Why do I feel closer to God in nature than when I'm with people or even at church?" I can hear the guilt in my coaching client's voice as she asks this question. We've been taught that we're to find God in buildings and with people, not under the stars or on a walk alone in the woods. Yet for many introverts, nature is the most sacred space in our lives.

God appeared to Moses through a burning bush in the wilderness. He whispered to the heart of David when the boy was a shepherd caring for a flock of sheep. He imparted truth to John on the beautiful island of Patmos. All these biblical characters appear to have been introverts, and they all heard God's voice in natural settings.

Scripture tells us, "The heavens proclaim the glory of God. The skies display his craftsmanship. Day after day they continue to speak; night after night they make him known. They speak without a sound or word; their voice is never heard. Yet their message has gone throughout the earth, and their words to all the world" (Ps. 19:1–4).

What are some of your favorite places in nature?

Why can introverts often hear God's voice when in nature? Because he speaks through his creation. Our introvert nervous systems also operate best in low-stimulation situations where less is coming at us from the outside. When we can block out the noise of modern life and return to the rhythms of the created world, it often opens us up to spiritual experiences.

We feel awe standing on the beach. We experience gratitude watching a beautiful sunset. We're reminded God is big and we are small when looking at the mountains. Our souls rediscover hope in the blooming of flowers, the hatching of eggs, the rainbow after a storm.

What's a time when you felt close to God in nature?

When we've lost touch with who we truly are, spending time in nature can be one of the most healing activities for us as introverts. It realigns us with God's original design. Studies have found that being in nature has psychological benefits such as decreased stress and an increased sense of well-being.[1] Don't have access to nature? Even imagining a scene like walking on the beach or resting under a tree can have the same effects.

SPENDING TIME IN *nature* CAN BE ONE OF THE MOST HEALING ACTIVITIES FOR US AS INTROVERTS.

As humans, our stories began in a garden, and they end with a new heaven and earth. Nature has always been part of God's plan, a way he reveals his goodness and character, a refuge and delight for our souls. He speaks to us through his creation if we will only quiet ourselves enough to listen. Introverts don't always need words to communicate—God doesn't either.

IN THIS MOMENT

BREATH PRAYER:
God, may I see and hear you
through your creation today.

Spend at least five minutes outside today. As you do, thank God for all that you see. Everything around you is a gift he's created for you to enjoy. You can record what you notice below.

I love to think of nature as an unlimited broadcasting station, through which God speaks to us every hour, if we will only tune in.

—GEORGE WASHINGTON CARVER

yesterday

A moment that filled me up was . . .

A moment that drained me was . . .

TA—DA! LIST

1. _____

2. _____

3. _____

today

One thing I'm worried about today is . . .

One thing I'm grateful for today is . . .

MY "DO WHAT YOU CAN" PLAN

1. _____

2. _____

3. _____

thoughts, feelings, ALL THE THINGS

nineteen

release false guilt

I'm sitting across from a fellow introvert in a lovely little coffee shop with white painted walls and the smell of espresso in the air. We're catching up on life, and she shares that she's struggling with how much of her time, energy, and emotion her kids need right now. "I shouldn't feel this way," she tells me.

I shouldn't feel . . .

I've heard so many other versions of this same story. The introvert in a corporate environment exhausted by endless meetings. The ministry leader who sometimes wants to lock the door and refuse to answer the phone ever again. The reluctant host at the holidays who would rather go freeze at the North Pole than have another family member show up for Christmas.

What do all these have in common? *False guilt.* We can detect false guilt by noticing when we use phrases like "I shouldn't feel this way" or "But I'm so grateful." Its presence is revealed when the wearier we get, the louder our inner critic becomes.

As introverts, we're given a lot of messages about what we should want, enjoy, or be capable of doing. The only problem is, even in church, those are usually coming from an extroverted culture. They don't align with who God created us to be; so here's your permission slip to stop feeling guilty.

When you feel overwhelmed by people, need time alone, or don't find something fun when other people do, *there is nothing wrong with you.* If you get tired of being around people, it simply means you've reached your body's and your mind's "done" point. If you crave solitude, remember that intentionally being alone isn't selfish; it's part of choosing to fill back up so that you can serve for a lifetime. If you don't jump up and down with excitement when others do, that's totally okay. It just means you're wired for joy in a different way.

And remember, half the world is wired like you. You are not the only one who feels like you do. Other moms get overwhelmed. Other employees are sick of meetings. Other ministry leaders sometimes want to run away to a deserted island. Other family members long for silent nights at Christmas.

Yes, sometimes God's Spirit does convict us of things we need to change. But that's different from false guilt.

False guilt tells us we are BAD; the Spirit reminds us to live as God's BELOVED.

False guilt tells us we need to MEET EXPECTATIONS; the Spirit always leads us back toward GRACE.

False guilt ACCUSES us; the Spirit AFFIRMS us.

False guilt tells us to TRY HARDER; the Spirit invites us to TRUST God in all things.

False guilt WEARS US DOWN; the Spirit BUILDS US UP.

"There is no condemnation for those who belong to Christ Jesus" (Rom. 8:1). As introverts, we can let go of false guilt and take hold of God's unending grace today.

IN THIS MOMENT

BREATH PRAYER:
God, there is no condemnation
for me because I belong to Christ Jesus.

Notice when you tell yourself "I shouldn't feel this way" today. Pause and say, "This is false guilt, and I choose to live in grace instead." What are you feeling right now that needs to be expressed and embraced?

_____

_____

_____

_____

_____

_____

_____

_____

God hasn't given us a spirit of fear or self-condemnation. . . . Let's practice leaning into appreciation instead of guilt and stop apologizing for who we are. Because, friends, every part of us is unsurprising to Him.

—ANNA E. RENDELL

yesterday

A moment that filled me up was . . .

A moment that drained me was . . .

TA—DA! LIST

1. _____

2. _____

3. _____

today

One thing I'm worried about today is . . .

One thing I'm grateful for today is . . .

MY "DO WHAT YOU CAN" PLAN

1. _____

2. _____

3. _____

thoughts, feelings, ALL THE THINGS

twenty

welcome a new perspective

"Fix your thoughts on what is *true,* and honorable, and right, and pure, and lovely, and admirable. Think about things that are *excellent* and worthy of *praise*" (PHIL. 4:8).

"Fix your thoughts . . ." When the apostle Paul wrote these words, he didn't mean to repair what's broken. Instead, *fix* here means to focus our thoughts in a consistent, intentional way. We, as introverts, have a natural strength for being aware of our internal words. But unless we're intentional about controlling our minds, our thoughts can go in unwanted directions.

What do you picture when you hear each of these words?

True

Honorable

Right

Pure

Lovely _____

Admirable _____

We all know what it's like to feel as though our minds are all over the place, jumping from one thought to another. We also have a negativity bias, which means we naturally notice what's wrong more than what's right in our lives. This helps with our survival; if a bear came charging into the coffee shop where I'm working, I'd notice it. But left unchecked, our negativity bias means our thoughts drift toward the opposite of what Paul said.

So how do we retrain our introvert brains? One simple way is through visualization. Think of the last time you worried. Maybe you pictured losing your job, a loved one getting into a car wreck, or a doctor sharing a terrible diagnosis with you. If you've ever had thoughts like these, you _already_ visualize. To visualize simply means to picture something in our minds. What helps us as introverts is learning to do so in constructive rather than destructive ways.

Visualization is powerful because of the way God created our brains. Neuropsychologist Amy Palmer explains, "The brain has the same activity when it visualizes doing an action as it does when it is physically performing the action."[1] (This is why consistent negative thinking can be harmful to our health and happiness; our brains and bodies react as if the terrible things we imagine are actually happening to us.)

Visualization engages the Reticular Activating System (RAS), an area of our brains that acts as a filter. Our RAS determines what we pay attention to, and it naturally prioritizes two things: threats and what we tell it is relevant. For example, if you decide to shop for a new red car, you'll likely start seeing red cars everywhere. Were they there before?

Of course, but your RAS labeled them as irrelevant, so you didn't really notice them.

When we visualize, it tells our RAS what we want it to notice. So if we practice picturing what is true, honorable, right, pure, lovely, and admirable, "things that are excellent and worthy of praise," then we'll start changing our thoughts.

Every morning I spend a few minutes visualizing a room full of people I love. I walk around and give each one a hug. Sometimes I picture Jesus in the room too. I engage all my senses—what do I see, hear, smell, touch, even taste? The more details I can add, the more my brain will engage. This exercise reminds me that everything I do that day is about loving God, others, and myself. It helps me live from a place of belonging and grace, which also significantly decreases my anxiety.

What's a place that brings you joy? Imagine it, then describe it below.

If I find myself getting anxious later in the day, I sometimes do a second visualization. I pause and picture myself on the beach where my family often goes for vacation, my favorite place in the world. I see the waves, hear the seagulls, smell the sea, feel the sand beneath my feet, and taste the salty air on my lips. As I imagine sitting on the beach, I go through the alphabet and say a name of God for each letter. This helps me remember that no matter what happens, I'll be okay, because God is good and he's taking care of not only me but the whole world too.

As you visualize, ask God for scenes that will re-align your thoughts, calm your mind, and draw you closer to him. *What we focus on, we will go toward in life*. We can drift into negativity or intentionally redirect our thoughts to what is life-giving, heart-freeing, and true.

WHAT WE
focus ON,
WE WILL
GO TOWARD
IN LIFE.

IN THIS MOMENT

BREATH PRAYER:
God, focus my thoughts on what is true,
honorable, right, pure, lovely, excellent,
and worthy of praise today.

Find a quiet place where you can sit upright, and then start a timer for five minutes. Picture your room of belonging. Hug each person in it and imagine they say something encouraging to you. Who do you see? What do you hear?

When our eyes are lifted high by Him, we gain a new perspective.

—PATRICIA RAYBON

yesterday

A moment that filled me up was . . .

A moment that drained me was . . .

TA—DA! LIST

1. _____

_____

2. _____

_____

3. _____

_____

today

One thing I'm worried about today is . . .

One thing I'm grateful for today is . . .

MY "DO WHAT YOU CAN" PLAN

1. _____

_____

2. _____

_____

3. _____

_____

thoughts, feelings, ALL THE THINGS

twenty-one

use your hands, heart, head

The dinner table is covered with food—meat hot off the grill, roasted vegetables, delicious potatoes, fruit cobbler. It's a feast, and we sit down to share it with several people we love. The conversation drifts between topics until the subject of relationships comes up. One person remarks, "I don't connect well with people."

She's an introvert, and I can see where on the surface this feels true to her sometimes. But something about her comment seems inaccurate and incomplete. It lingers in my mind long after we clear the dishes, and eventually I put words to the deeper truth: she is good at connecting with people, she just does it in her own way.

What are some of your favorite ways to serve people?

That evening she brought a handmade gift she'd thoughtfully crafted for someone. She's an amazing cook and loves feeding her people. If you have a practical need, she's there to meet it. She's excellent at connecting with her hands.

I can provide empathy, support, and understanding. But you don't want me in charge of your menu, fixing anything that's broken in your house, or healing any part of your body. I connect well with my heart but struggle sometimes to connect with my hands.

My husband, Mark, is the one you want when you have an issue involving numbers, need an efficient plan, or are looking for a well-researched solution. I trust his judgment and seek his wisdom, and people in our life often come to him for business advice. Mark connects with others primarily through his head rather than his hands or heart.

Which do you most naturally serve with? Circle it here.

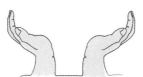

Of course, we use all three (hands, heart, head) at different times. But as introverts, we might find it helpful to know there's one that comes more naturally to us. If we don't understand this, we can make the mistake of believing we're not good at connecting with people when the opposite is true.

Your unique way of serving others is needed. Our world would be out of balance without it. We need introverts with gifted hands. We need introverts with tender hearts. We need introverts with insightful minds. As Peter said,

"God has given each of you some special *abilities*; be sure to use them to help each other, passing on to others God's many kinds of *blessings*" (1 PET. 4:10 TLB).

IN THIS MOMENT

BREATH PRAYER:
God, you've gifted me to connect
with and serve others. Use me today.

Sometimes we don't even realize how we're serving because it comes so naturally to us. Today keep a list of each way you help someone, no matter how small or insignificant it may seem. What's little to us can be a big deal to others and to God.

My prayer is that you would be encouraged to build community, make connections, and serve as you live out God's unique purpose for you.

—JESS ADKINS

yesterday

A moment that filled me up was . . .

.

A moment that drained me was . . .

today

One thing I'm worried about today is . . .

One thing I'm grateful for today is . . .

TA–DA! LIST

1. _____

_____

2. _____

_____

3. _____

_____

MY "DO WHAT YOU CAN" PLAN

1. _____

_____

2. _____

_____

3. _____

_____

thoughts, feelings, ALL THE THINGS

twenty-two

live with powerful humility

I'm standing at the front of a room with tables full of people, explaining that we're about to go through exercises to help us figure out our strengths, skills, and who God made us. I notice a worried look in the back corner, followed by a hand quietly raised and a question asked. "I want to do this, but I'm afraid it's not humble. What if I'm being prideful?"

In Your Words

Humility means

Pride means

I can certainly understand that concern, because I struggled with a fear of accidentally "becoming prideful" for many years. It bothered me so much, I finally decided to look at Scripture to see what true humility means. Most of the time, the word *humility* is from the Hebrew word *Kana*, which implies submission to another's will. In the New Testament, it's a Greek word formed from two others: *tapeinos* (low to the ground) and *phren* (our hearts/minds).

Put all that together and we see that *humility means bowing our hearts to God*. Or in other words, submitting to his will. And that means agreeing with what he says and living it out—including what he says about us. Our strengths and skills are more than personal characteristics; they're messages that tell us who God made us.

It's never God's intention for us as introverts to go through life with our heads hanging down in insecurity and our hearts made heavy by the fear that we're not enough. We come to God and say, "I bow my heart before you in love. You are God and I am not. All I am, all I have, is yours." Then he responds, "Stand tall, my child. You are loved. You are of great worth. I have a plan and purpose for you."

> "*Humble* yourselves before the Lord,
> and he will *lift* you up" (JAMES 4:10).

Sometimes as introverts we mistake insecurity for humility, but the two are very different.

Insecurity pushes us DOWN; humility lifts us UP.

Insecurity causes us to HIDE; humility helps us
SHOW UP as we are without pretending.

Insecurity whispers, "You CAN'T do it"; humility
reminds us that with God, ANYTHING IS POSSIBLE.

Insecurity tells us we need to CHANGE who we are;
humility invites us to BECOME more of who God
truly made us.

Insecurity reminds us of our FLAWS; humility
encourages us to use our STRENGTHS and gifts
to serve.

Insecurity COMPARES us to others; humility reminds
us God has a UNIQUE purpose for our lives.

Insecurity tells us being an introvert isn't ENOUGH;
humility says we have EVERYTHING WE NEED
because God has given it to us.

Today, let's not live with pride or insecurity but with true and grateful
humility.

IN THIS MOMENT

God, help me see myself as you see me today.

Which do you tend to struggle with more—pride or insecurity? What helps you live with true humility instead?

_____

_____

_____

_____

_____

_____

_____

_____

_____

_____

Jesus is the only One who can meet our deepest need to be known, accepted, and pursued simply because of who we are.

—RENEE SWOPE

yesterday

A moment that filled me up was . . .

A moment that drained me was . . .

TA–DA! LIST

1. _____

_____

2. _____

_____

3. _____

_____

today

One thing I'm worried about today is . . .

One thing I'm grateful for today is . . .

MY "DO WHAT YOU CAN" PLAN

1. _____

_____

2. _____

_____

3. _____

_____

thoughts, feelings, ALL THE THINGS

twenty-three

be a noticer of others

A dear friend recently told me a touching story about his daughter. A peer of hers—someone popular and beautiful, confident and always included—had a brain tumor that left her with a slur and a lopsided face. In the time when she needed them most, all her "friends" faded away. But my friend's daughter sought her out, helped her see that her inner worth hadn't changed just because her external appearance had. She was still beloved, and she still had a place to belong.

Not surprisingly, my friend's daughter is an introvert. One of the greatest strengths of introverts is noticing those others may overlook or dismiss. This is partly because of our powers of perception—we see the one person sitting alone at lunch, how she's nervously fiddling with her napkin, the way she looks down to avoid attention but at the same time desperately hopes someone will notice her.

Who is your heart drawn to when you're in a room full of people?

We, as introverts, often understand what it's like to feel out of place. In our extrovert-centric culture, we've likely experienced moments of being misunderstood, underestimated, or unseen. This gives us empathy for others who might not fit in the way they sometimes long to either. "Love one another" (1 John 3:23).

When I look at the life of Jesus, I see him noticing those whom others might overlook too. In a familiar story, he's traveling with his disciples through the village of Samaria. He stops to rest at noontime, and a woman arrives at the local well. Scholars speculate this woman came to the well at noon during the heat of the day to avoid the other women in her village. She's had five husbands and is living with a sixth man. She's an outcast to not only the Jews but also her own people—another popular girl whose "friends" and men have disappeared. She certainly doesn't expect a Jewish man to show her respect: "The woman was surprised, for Jews refuse to have anything to do with Samaritans" (John 4:9).

What's a time when someone engaged with you in an encouraging way?

Jesus not only reaches out to her, but he also validates her worth. He asks her for a drink; *you have something to offer*. He engages her in conversation; *you are worth seeing and listening to*. She's the first person Jesus directly tells he is the Messiah, and he allows her to tell others about him too; *you are valuable, and God can still use you.*

As introverts, we may not be the center of attention, but we may very well be the one God sends to the person in the room who *needs* the most attention. Never underestimate your introvert gift of noticing those who others might overlook. It reflects the heart of the God who sees us, knows us, and reminds us of our worth. This kind of love is more than popular or loud; it's powerful and life changing.

IN THIS MOMENT

BREATH PRAYER:
God, may I see others the way you do today.

Who's one person in your life who might feel overlooked? What's one small way you can remind them of their worth today?

_____

_____

_____

_____

_____

_____

_____

_____

_____

_____

God loves his people *through* his people.

—SHANNAN MARTIN

yesterday

today

A moment that filled me up was . . .

One thing I'm worried about today is . . .

A moment that drained me was . . .

One thing I'm grateful for today is . . .

TA—DA! LIST

MY "DO WHAT YOU CAN" PLAN

1. _____

2. _____

3. _____

1. _____

2. _____

3. _____

thoughts, feelings, ALL THE THINGS

twenty-four
seek true transformation

I'm sitting at a round table in an old house that's been turned into a little bakery. Two friends are with me. We have a mastermind group in which we talk about work, life, and spirituality. As we sip coffee and eat our treats, the topic turns to one we all wrestle with—*how do we truly change?*

By nature, I'm a try-harder, do-better, give-me-the-gold-star person. Set a standard or imply an expectation, and I'll work to meet it. This behavior isn't always healthy—and I have to keep a close eye on it—but it is my reality.

When have you tried to change who you are?

What's one way God is helping you embrace who he made you to be?

When I decided being an introvert might not be sufficient, I set out to change who I was. If something felt hard or uncomfortable to me, I just did it anyway. I thought losing my true self was the price I had to pay for success. Unsurprisingly, I pushed myself to the brink of burnout. As I've shared, this led me to reconnect with who God made me as an introvert. But this "new me" sometimes dug in her heels and stubbornly refused to adapt for anything or anyone. If something was hard or uncomfortable, I avoided it.

WE CAN change OR NOT CHANGE, BUT ONLY GOD CAN transform US.

Does this sound familiar? On this morning with my friends, we talk about similar situations in our lives, times when we've tried to change or resisted doing so. Then right there in that little bakery we have what feels like a holy moment, and these unexpected, heart-freeing words come out of my mouth: "We can change or not change, but only God can transform us."

Change is EXTERNAL; transformation is INTERNAL.

Change is about our EFFORTS; transformation is about GOD'S WORK IN US.

Change is about TRYING; transformation is about YIELDING.

Change is about what we DO or DON'T DO; transformation is about who we're BECOMING.

Change is _____;

transformation is _____.

One of my biggest goals in writing about introverts is that we will no longer feel pressure to change who we are. But one of my biggest fears is that embracing who we are will cause us to say, "Great! Now I have an excuse not to do anything outside my comfort zone. I am who I am, and everyone else just has to deal with it." Instead, I want our understanding of who we are as introverts to help us stop focusing on change either way and become more intentional about asking God for true transformation.

The process of transformation that God invites us into isn't something we can accomplish or do. It's not about self-help or personal improvement. It's about yielding all of who we are to who God is so he can make us more like him, which also means we become more of our truest, deepest, and most eternal selves.

Transformation always leads us to become more loving and grace-filled because "God is love" (1 John 4:8). How we express that love will differ for each of us, but the invitation is the same—to be made more like the God who made us.

IN THIS MOMENT

BREATH PRAYER:
God, you are the source of true transformation.
Work in and through me as only you can.

When do you sometimes resist needed change or stepping outside
your comfort zone? What helps you when that happens?

_____

_____

_____

_____

_____

_____

_____

_____

_____

_____

I want to help you to grow as beautiful as God meant you to be when he
thought of you first.

—GEORGE MACDONALD

yesterday

A moment that filled me up was . . .

A moment that drained me was . . .

TA—DA! LIST

1.

2.

3.

today

One thing I'm worried about today is . . .

One thing I'm grateful for today is . . .

MY "DO WHAT YOU CAN" PLAN

1.

2.

3.

thoughts, feelings, ALL THE THINGS

twenty-five
find your hiding place

It's a gray winter day with clouds, like a quilt, laid over everything. I'm half awake as I slide into the driver's seat of my car to head to a local coffee shop for a morning of writing. I press Play on a new podcast a friend has recommended. I hear introvert, author, and singer Christy Nockels, who has a voice like honey and light, talk about what it means to find a hiding place in God.

She shares how years ago a friend of hers described this place like the center of a bull's-eye. We serve and do in the outer rings. But the center, she says, "is where we're fully known as beloved by God. Inside the bull's-eye, this is who you are. It's the place you do everything from."[1] I take a deep breath, and my eyes pop open as if I've downed a shot of espresso.

"You are my *hiding place*;
> you will protect me from trouble
> and surround me with songs of deliverance" (PS. 32:7 NIV).

Just last night I curled under layers of covers. A comforter, blanket, another blanket. Two pillows. I burrowed down into my bed and closed my eyes. It had been a tough day, and I thought of how modern life, especially social media, sometimes leaves me feeling overexposed as an introvert.

When do you feel the need to hide?

I reflected on the legacy of my grandparents, who owned a small Christian bookstore in a little town and served simply and quietly for a lifetime. I whispered a paradox prayer: "Use me. Hide me." Whether it's in our work, personal circumstances, or relationships, we all have moments of feeling overwhelmed and vulnerable.

Yet it's still hard for me to utter this short prayer because I've always thought of hiding as somehow bad. We live in a go-out-there-and-be-bold kind of world. But it seems a longing for hiding is built into us. We tuck our faces into the necks of our parents as babies. We play hide-and-seek with our childhood friends. As adults we hide in less conspicuous ways—behind the screen of a computer, in the bottom of a glass, underneath all that makeup. So perhaps it's not about whether we will hide but rather where and how.

GOD HIMSELF SAYS HE WILL BE OUR *hiding place.*

And this is the beautiful reality: God himself says he will be our hiding place. He will be the retreat and the fortress and the silent space in a chaotic, busy world.

How is God your hiding place?

Christy goes on to say, "When we hide in the place that's already been carved out for us to hide in, we emerge from that place our truest selves."[2] In other words, when we find our refuge in God, we can be who we are, do what we're called to do, and live without shame and guilt and fear.

When Adam and Eve fell, they hid. God came looking for them and asked, "Where are you?" (Gen. 3:9). It seems like a strange question because, as God, he already knew. Perhaps he needed to ask because *they* didn't fully realize the truth. Maybe he is asking the same of us today: *Where are you?*

No matter the answer we may give—"in the middle of depression," "on the battlefield," "at the center of a stage"—he wants us to know that is not our truest, deepest location. Where we belong, where we've been all along, where we always are in some mysterious way is *in him*. Secure. Loved. Known. He is our hiding place; he is our heart's true home.

IN THIS MOMENT

BREATH PRAYER:
God, no matter where I am or what I do,
I am always secure and cared for in you.

What's a time when hiding was a delight, like playing hide-and-seek or reading under the covers?

_____

_____

_____

_____

_____

_____

_____

_____

In my quest to experience space for my soul, to pin it down and plan for it, I'm hearing a voice remind me that it isn't simply space I want. It's Jesus. I want the calm and strength and understanding only he provides. I want to be known fully, loved wholly, accepted unconditionally. That is really what I want.

—EMILY P. FREEMAN

yesterday

A moment that filled me up was . . .

A moment that drained me was . . .

TA–DA! LIST

1. _____

_____

2. _____

_____

3. _____

_____

today

One thing I'm worried about today is . . .

One thing I'm grateful for today is . . .

MY "DO WHAT YOU CAN" PLAN

1. _____

_____

2. _____

_____

3. _____

_____

thoughts, feelings, ALL THE THINGS

twenty-six

keep your courage

As an introvert, you might have days when you battle discouragement. Why? Because you experience the world deeply. You're affected by what's going on around you. You're impacted by the people you love. You think intentionally and process thoroughly. When you live like this in a world that's not always kind, where hard things happen every day, sometimes you're not going to feel okay about it all.

Discourage simply means to lose courage. For us as introverts, that can feel like losing our desire to show up, open our hearts, let people into our lives, pursue our dreams, or believe that tomorrow can be better than today. We might even find ourselves wishing everything and everyone would just go away.

What helps you keep your courage?

So what do we need in those moments? Many of the things we've talked about, such as rest and soul-filling activities like solitude. But I've come to see that we also need to be able to say to at least one person: "I'm feeling discouraged today."

A dear friend of mine said this to me yesterday, and I understood because I was discouraged too. We asked each other, "How do we make a plan to help each other through days like this?" Sometimes when we're down, it can be hard to come up with the words to express how we're feeling. We decided we'd have a code word to make it easy to tell each other when we were feeling this way. This word can be silly like *taco* or *penguin*, serious like *help* or *sinking*, or somewhere in between.

Who encourages you?

Who do you encourage?

We talked about how if one of us said this word, it meant we needed a safe space to be human. We weren't asking to be fixed or rescued, and we weren't saying our discouragement was the other person's fault. Then we brainstormed a question we would ask each other as a follow-up whenever one of us used this code word. We decided on "How can I best support you right now?" The answer might be . . .

I need to process X.

I need help with Y.

I need a new perspective on Z.

Or something else entirely.

Discouragement isn't a sign of weakness; it's proof we're warriors who are alive and engaged, who sometimes get weary or wounded. God invites us to encourage each other because he knows this world is a hard place to be sometimes.

Getting discouraged is inevitable; fighting it alone is optional.

"So *encourage* each other
and build each other up, just as you
are already doing" (1 THESS. 5:11).

IN THIS MOMENT

BREATH PRAYER:
God, you are an encourager.
Make me one today too.

Think of one person you can encourage today and do so. Also think of one person who can encourage you and let them know what you need.

_____

_____

_____

_____

_____

_____

_____

_____

_____

_____

No matter how old we get or how strong we've grown, we can all use encouragement.

—BONNIE GRAY

yesterday

A moment that filled me up was . . .

A moment that drained me was . . .

TA—DA! LIST

1. _____

   _____

2. _____

   _____

3. _____

   _____

today

One thing I'm worried about today is . . .

One thing I'm grateful for today is . . .

MY "DO WHAT YOU CAN" PLAN

1. _____

   _____

2. _____

   _____

3. _____

   _____

thoughts, feelings, ALL THE THINGS

twenty-seven

live between possibility and potential

As introverts, one of our superpowers is seeing potential. This shows up in different ways, depending on our individual personalities and gifts. For example, an accountant sees the potential in an investment, a coach the potential in an athlete, a chef the potential in an ordinary potato, a counselor the potential in a broken person.

Potential starts with perception, the feeling we get as introverts that whispers to us, "There's a possibility here." This may happen in a conversation, when we're walking through the aisles of a craft store, or while we're doing research at work. We feel compelled to chase those possibilities, to turn what we imagine into reality.

What's a time when you saw potential in an idea, project, or person? What did you do to help bring that potential into being?

One of the most powerful ways introverts add value to our world is by seeing what can be. Dr. Elaine Aron says about people with high perception:

> We are the writers, historians, philosophers, judges, artists, researchers, theologians, therapists, teachers, parents, and plain conscientious citizens. What we bring to any of these roles is a tendency to THINK ABOUT ALL THE POSSIBLE EFFECTS of an idea.[1]

Our gift of perception can sometimes trip us up when we think we can go from perceiving a possibility to achieving full potential right away. I've worked with many coaching clients who say, "I think I can write a book" (possibility). But then when they sit down in front of a computer and it's hard to write, life gets hectic, or they compare themselves to other authors, they give up. "I must have been wrong," they say. "I can't write a book after all."

What they don't realize (and we work through together) is that seeing potential is a starting point of a process with many steps. We still need to plan, practice, and persevere until what we envision becomes reality. When we forget this, we often tell ourselves we're failures because we're not yet where we want to be. Or when we see unreached potential in people or projects, we get discouraged and frustrated.

POTENTIAL (Where We Want to Be)

PROGRESS (Where We Are Today)

POSSIBILITY (Hope, Desire, or Dream)

We can remind ourselves, *there is always a gap between possibility and potential.* If we're describing something that's within our control, like writing a book, then we can make a practical plan to close that gap. If it's not within our control, like the choices of another person, then we can release them from our expectations and extend grace. (One exception would be destructive behavior, like abuse or addiction, and then we need to make our personal safety and well-being the priority.)

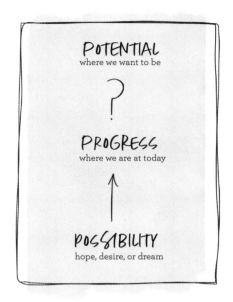

POTENTIAL
where we want to be

?

PROGRESS
where we are at today

POSSIBILITY
hope, desire, or dream

When Jesus first met Peter, he changed his name to Cephas, which means "rock" in the original language. But all throughout the Gospels, Peter seems like anything but a rock. He's impulsive and unstable, and he even denies Jesus in a time of crisis. Yet Jesus doesn't dismiss Peter. Instead, he keeps encouraging, training, and forgiving him until Peter eventually becomes the leader Jesus always knew he could be.

Without care and attention, our ability as introverts to see potential can be a stumbling block that gets in the way. But when we use this gift intentionally, it can be a stepping stone to greatness for ourselves and others. "I am certain that God, who began the good work within you, will continue his work until it is finally finished on the day when Christ Jesus returns" (Phil. 1:6).

Look around you. So much of what you see that's beautiful and innovative, heart healing and world changing, started as a thought in the mind of one introvert who had the courage and perseverance to make it a reality.

IN THIS MOMENT

What's a possibility you see right now? Write down one small step you can take toward turning it into a reality.

_____

_____

_____

_____

_____

_____

_____

_____

_____

Mighty oaks from little acorns grow.

—fourteenth-century ENGLISH PROVERB

yesterday

A moment that filled me up was . . .

A moment that drained me was . . .

TA–DA! LIST

1. _____

   _____

2. _____

   _____

3. _____

   _____

today

One thing I'm worried about today is . . .

One thing I'm grateful for today is . . .

MY "DO WHAT YOU CAN" PLAN

1. _____

   _____

2. _____

   _____

3. _____

   _____

thoughts, feelings, ALL THE THINGS

twenty-eight
know you have nothing to prove

As an introvert, I'm learning to listen to my body, to let it tell me when I'm tired or anxious, when I feel safe in a person's presence or need to watch out, when something sparks joy in me or drains my internal battery. For years I ignored the wisdom in my body. I pushed too hard. I went too far. I held on too long. And all the while, my body was trying to tell me *something is wrong.*

When I'm happy, my body feels _____

_____

When I'm sad, my body feels _____

_____

When I'm anxious or afraid, my body feels _____

_____

When we don't listen to our bodies, it's usually because we're trying to live up to someone else's expectations. We tell ourselves we should be able to do more. We should be able to go faster. We should be able to live as mechanical robots rather than introvert masterpieces who are made for quality over quantity, distance over speed, and depth over busy-busy distraction.

I was reminded of this on my run this morning. My training app gave me a new goal, but as I neared the end of my workout, I felt my body begin to say, "You need to stop." I'm all for pushing hard, sweating it out, and challenging myself to do more than I think I can. But sometimes there comes a moment when my body truly does mean it, when I've hit my "done" point. If I keep going, I'm not getting stronger; I'm only risking injury.

How do you know when you've hit your "done" point as an introvert?

I didn't want to listen, of course, but I remembered an article on a running website that talked about having the mental maturity to rest. Some of us struggle to get going, but others of us find it much harder to stop. I'm among the latter. Today I yielded and slowed to a walk. As soon as I did, I sensed a wise whisper in my soul that said, "You have nothing to prove—even to yourself." It's interesting to me that when I listen to my body, it often provides space for God's Spirit to speak too. I needed to remember this simple truth:

"Christ has *accepted* you" (ROM. 15:7).

As introverts, we often feel we do have something to prove. We want people to know we're likable even if we're not the life of the party. We have something to contribute even if we're not the chattiest person in the meeting. We have something to offer the world even if we're reluctant to stand on a stage. This desire to prove ourselves is often what pushes us to act like extroverts, to run and run until we're exhausted, then run some more.

We, too, need the mental maturity to slow down and remember our true identity. We are beloved by God. We are needed in this world just as we are. We have strengths to share, insights to offer, quiet gifts of great value to place in the lives, hearts, and hands of those around us. When we ignore all this and persist in our pursuit of what doesn't align with who we truly are, we risk injury too.

Sometimes other people put pressure on us. But I've found as introverts, we're often the ones forcing ourselves to keep going, refusing to stop, fearing rejection is always right at our heels and if we slow down at all it will catch us. This is an exhausting way to live. I've had enough of it. I imagine you have too.

Let's listen to our introvert bodies when they tell us we've reached our "done" point. Let's have the mental maturity to embrace a different pace. Let's dare to create space for our souls to hear what has always been true: *we have nothing to prove—even to ourselves.*

IN THIS MOMENT

BREATH PRAYER:
God, I am loved by you,
and I have nothing to prove today.

Pause and do a body scan. Close your eyes and shift your attention from the top of your head down to the bottom of your feet. Where are you relaxed? Where do you feel tension?

_____

_____

_____

_____

_____

_____

_____

_____

_____

Christ continually shouts through the universe, "You have a love that is already yours. You have nothing to prove to anyone. You have nothing to prove to Me. You are significant and preapproved and utterly cherished. Not because you are 'good,' but because you are Mine."

—JENNIFER DUKES LEE

yesterday

A moment that filled me up was . . .

A moment that drained me was . . .

today

One thing I'm worried about today is . . .

One thing I'm grateful for today is . . .

TA—DA! LIST

1. _____

_____

2. _____

_____

3. _____

_____

MY "DO WHAT YOU CAN" PLAN

1. _____

_____

2. _____

_____

3. _____

_____

thoughts, feelings, ALL THE THINGS

twenty-nine

listen to the gentle whisper of god

I spent years avoiding my true self, chasing external rewards instead of choosing internal peace, overlooking my introvert strengths, and only seeing my very human struggles. I'd like to go back to my awkward, anxious younger self and tell her, "You have nothing to prove. You're already loved. You're already enough."

I wish I'd had the courage back then to listen to the whisper of God more often instead of the noisy-noisy world telling me who I should be. When I finally decided to listen to God, a story about his whisper helped me change my perspective on my purpose as an introvert.

The prophet Elijah is struggling with insecurity and discouragement. He feels exhausted and alone.

"Go out and stand before me on the mountain," the LORD told him. And as Elijah stood there, the LORD passed by, and a mighty windstorm hit the mountain. It was such a terrible blast that the rocks were torn loose, but the LORD was not in the wind. After the wind there was an earthquake, but the LORD was not in the earthquake. And after the earthquake there was a fire, but the LORD was not in the fire. And after the fire there was the sound of a GENTLE WHISPER.[1]

I, too, looked for God in the wind—in activity, busyness, hustling to prove my worth. It almost tore my life apart. I did the same through what felt like an inner earthquake, splitting my true self into pieces so I could get approval, never really feeling steady or sure. I've tried fire, the flash of performance, efforts to impress. But what I really needed all along was a gentle whisper.

What is God whispering to your heart?

When I finally started listening to the whisper of God, I also began finding sustainable peace, my real purpose, the voice that tells me I am loved and enough as is, not as I think I ought to be. I feel so grateful for how far that voice has brought me. Now I want to be a voice who helps others embrace who they are as introverts too, and I imagine you share that desire.

We can tell ourselves we need to be louder or more outgoing or that we should change who we are. But what if we, as introverts, are created to be living echoes of the gentle whisper of God? What if that's why the world needs us to be who we are? What if that's our powerful purpose?

No one needs more empty noise. What we all need is more love—and that can come through the gentle whisper of God through the powerful echo we can be as introverts.

IN THIS MOMENT

BREATH PRAYER:
God, may I be a living echo of your
gentle whisper in a noisy world.

What are three things you want to remember from your journey through this journal?

I want to remember . . .

1. _____

   _____

   _____

2. _____

   _____

   _____

3. _____

   _____

   _____

God does not shout; he whispers, and in that whisper is the way.

—DEAN KOONTZ

yesterday

A moment that filled me up was . . .

A moment that drained me was . . .

I. _____

_____

2. _____

_____

3. _____

_____

today

One thing I'm worried about today is . . .

One thing I'm grateful for today is . . .

MY "DO WHAT YOU CAN" PLAN

I. _____

_____

2. _____

_____

3. _____

_____

thoughts, feelings, ALL THE THINGS

thirty

do what no one else does

"Most people don't . . ."

Those three words *ping* in my mind over and over like pebbles against a glass window. When they do, I pause and consider, "It's true. Most people don't spend so much time sitting in front of a laptop and writing." And then it comes: "What's the matter with you? Why be more like most people?"

You've had these words thrown like stones at you too, haven't you?

Most people don't . . . wear themselves out in the kitchen because they believe a meal feeds hearts and fills bellies.

Most people don't . . . throw off their entire schedule because they take time to listen to the stranger in the grocery store who's having a hard day.

Most people don't . . . pore over spreadsheets until their eyes are red because they see numbers as a sort of art and a way of bringing order to a chaotic world.

What do you do that most people don't?

It's true. Most people don't do what you do, love what you love, feel the kind of passion you feel about that thing.

I started thinking about this recently, and I realized we're in pretty good company if we feel like we're not like most people. After all:

Most people don't . . . build an ARK.

Most people don't . . . lead people through the desert to the PROMISED LAND.

Most people don't . . . die on a CROSS to save the world.

But aren't we glad ONE PERSON did each of these things?

As introverts, we can feel pressure to conform, but what makes the biggest impact is when we live out our God-given uniqueness instead. The world does not need copies; it needs originals. Your community doesn't need cookie-cutter people; it needs caring individuals who make a difference in small ways every day. Your work, school, or volunteer organization doesn't need one more person who just shows up; it needs someone who reflects the image of God like no one else ever has or ever will. The word *masterpiece* in Ephesians 2:10 can also be translated as "poem." Every poem is unique—an intentional, impactful work of creativity.

> "For we are God's *masterpiece.*
> He has created us anew in Christ Jesus,
> so we can do the *good things*
> he planned for us long ago" (EPH. 2:10).

If most people don't do what you do, and you're passionately pursuing Jesus with your life, then it's probably not just a human plan. The heartbeat of God is probably somewhere within it. We need you—just you—to fulfill that purpose, complete that project, bring that gift to the world in a way no one else can.

Most people don't . . . but, introvert, you do.

IN THIS MOMENT

What's one thing you'll do differently because of this journey?

_____

_____

_____

_____

_____

From now on, I will . . .

_____

_____

_____

_____

_____

Be who God meant you to be and you will set the world on fire.

—ST. CATHERINE OF SIENA

yesterday

A moment that filled me up was . . .

A moment that drained me was . . .

TA—DA! LIST

1. _____

2. _____

3. _____

today

One thing I'm worried about today is . . .

One thing I'm grateful for today is . . .

MY "DO WHAT YOU CAN" PLAN

1. _____

2. _____

3. _____

thoughts, feelings, ALL THE THINGS

thirty-one

trust you have enough for a lifetime

As an introvert, one of the lies I find myself sometimes battling is, "I don't have enough . . ." Maybe you can relate? The way I finish the sentence depends on the day.

I don't have enough energy.

I don't have enough words.

I don't have enough strength.

I don't have enough _____.

So how can we change what we say to ourselves?

I've been thinking of the story from the Gospels when Jesus feeds a huge crowd. As evening comes, the disciples tell him to dismiss everyone for a dinner break. There's no fast-food restaurant nearby, so Jesus responds that the disciples can feed the people. They protest, "But we have only five loaves of bread and two fish!" (Matt. 14:17).

One phrase sounds familiar to me: "But we have only . . ." In other words, "We don't have enough." The disciples respond this way because they see only the human side of the situation. But Jesus looks beyond this to the deeper reality.

What do you sometimes say to yourself?

But I have only _____ .

What if we pause and shift our perspective as introverts too? In my life, that sounds like . . .

- I don't have enough energy to do everything, but I have enough for what God is asking me to do today.
- I don't have enough words to talk nonstop, but I have enough to make meaningful connections.
- I don't have enough strength to be all things to all people, but I have enough to love well and fulfill God's purpose for me.
- I don't have enough _____ , but I have enough _____ .

What would your version be? If what we have to offer feels as small as five loaves and two fish, that's okay. It's not how much we have that matters; it's Whose hands we place it in today.

You, introvert, have strengths, skills, and gifts to offer this world. You're a quiet, powerful presence who's needed more than ever before. You have the capacity for meaningful connections, deep thinking, and embracing soul-filling solitude. Sometimes our noisy, chaotic world may feel overwhelming, but don't ever let that convince you that you have less to offer than extroverts.

Not only do you have enough, but you *are* enough. The God who spoke the world into being also knows your name, numbers every hair on your head, and understands every care in your heart. He created you to be irreplaceable, a wonder and a miracle—even on the days when you don't feel like it. Just because you don't always see yourself that way doesn't mean it isn't true. You reflect the image of God as no one else can and no one else ever will.

"This same God who *takes care* of me
will supply all your needs
from his *glorious riches*,
which have been given to us in Christ Jesus" (PHIL. 4:19).

So, introvert, dare to be who God created you to be. Trust that he will give you all that you need for his purpose for your life. Resist the urge to conform and instead fully offer your quiet, powerful uniqueness. In God's hands, it will be exactly what someone needs today.

IN THIS MOMENT

BREATH PRAYER:
God, I place who I am
and all I have in your hands today.

What are your "loaves and fish"? What can you offer as an introvert? Write your answers in the spaces provided.

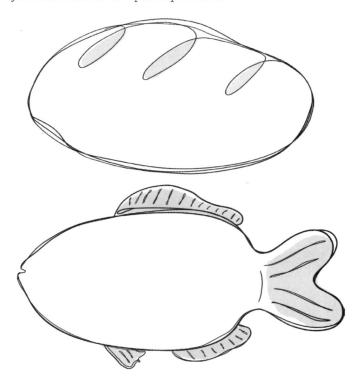

Let's walk together and treat each person like an image bearer of God to be treasured.

—DORINA LAZO GILMORE—YOUNG

yesterday

A moment that filled me up was . . .

A moment that drained me was . . .

1. _____

_____

2. _____

_____

3. _____

_____

today

One thing I'm worried about today is . . .

One thing I'm grateful for today is . . .

MY "DO WHAT YOU CAN" PLAN

1. _____

_____

2. _____

_____

3. _____

_____

thoughts, feelings, ALL THE THINGS

more resources for you, introvert

Visit HolleyGerth.com/Introverts for more resources:

The Powerful Purpose of Introverts: Why the World Needs You to Be You (Book)
7 Ways to Thrive as an Introvert (Online course)
Your Introvert Coach (Free email newsletter)

And more!

acknowledgments

As an introvert, I don't like getting attention, but I love giving it.

First and most of all, to my husband, Mark, I love sharing life with a fellow introvert. I'm grateful for the quiet moments, the new adventures, and all the unexpected ways we complement each other.

To my editor, Jennifer Leep, thank you for over a decade of doing books together. You're not only the person whose perspective makes everything I write better, but you're also a dear and trusted friend.

To my wonderful team at Revell—especially Andrea Doering, Wendy Wetzel, Amy Ballor, Eileen Hanson, and Kelli Smith—I'm so grateful for the years we've spent together, and I look forward to what's ahead.

To my virtual assistant, Kaitlyn Bouchillon, your diligence, excellence, creativity, and friendship help more than you could ever know. I appreciate all you do.

Thank you to my friend and fellow creative thinker, Jason Rovenstine, for helping me make this journal better.

To Mom and Dad, thanks for teaching me that quietness is powerful, kindness is courageous, and becoming who you're created to be is life's greatest adventure.

To my grandmother, Eula Armstrong, you are an example of resilience and following Jesus for a lifetime. Thank you for all your prayers.

To my daughter, Lovelle, you're a gift, and God knew exactly what our family needed—a brave, bright-shining, joy-bringing, beautiful extrovert!

To my granddaughter, Eula, and grandson, Clement, I can't wait to see who God created you to be. You're already a delight.

To all my introvert and extrovert readers who responded to my survey, sent notes, or had conversations with me, thank you for helping shape *The Powerful Purpose of Introverts* and this journal through all the wisdom you offered, insights you gave, and stories you shared.

Most of all, to God, thank you for making us who we are. May we become all you've created us to be.

"I praise you because you made me
in an *amazing* and *wonderful* way.
What you have done is wonderful.
I know this very well" (PS. 139:14 ICB).

notes

Chapter 6 Remember You're Not the Only One

1. "How Frequent Is My Type," The Myers & Briggs Foundation, accessed August 4, 2022, https://www.myersbriggs.org/my-mbti-personality-type/my-mbti-results/how-frequent-is-my-type.htm.

2. The Myers-Briggs Company, "Setting the Record Straight on World Introvert Day: Introverts Make Great Leaders Too," news release, January 2, 2020, https://www.themyersbriggs.com/en-US/Company/Press/Press/2020/January/Setting-the-Record-Straight-on-World-Introvert-Day.

3. Tavi Gevinson, "I Want It to Be Worth It: An Interview with Emma Watson," *Rookie*, May 27, 2013, https://www.rookiemag.com/2013/05/emma-watson-interview/5/.

Chapter 7 See Struggles as the Other End of Strengths

1. Megan Malone, "For Introverts, Mindfulness Is the Key to Combating Negative Thoughts," Introvert, Dear, February 4, 2022, https://introvertdear.com/news/negative-thoughts-ruining-life/.

Chapter 8 Choose Quality over Quantity

1. 1 Cor. 13:4–7.

2. Brené Brown, *The Gifts of Imperfection: Let Go of Who You Think You're Supposed to Be and Embrace Who You Are* (Center City, MN: Hazelden Publishing, 2010), 26.

3. Holley Gerth, *Fiercehearted: Live Fully, Love Bravely* (Grand Rapids: Revell, 2017), 32.

Chapter 10 Dare to Show Up as You Are

1. Gen. 3:8–11.

Chapter 11 Know Your Influence Matters

1. Daniel Goleman, *Social Intelligence* (New York: Bantam, 2007), 5.

2. Brandon Cox, "The Best Personality Type for Ministry Leaders," Brandon A. Cox, accessed April 2, 2020, https://brandonacox.com/leadership-personality-type/.

3. Cox, "The Best Personality Type."

Chapter 12 Believe You Can Handle It

1. Susan Jeffers, *Feel the Fear and Do It Anyway: Dynamic Techniques for Turning Fear, Indecision, and Anger into Power, Action, and Love* (New York: Random House, 1987), 15.

Chapter 14 Overcome Overthinking

1. Jenn Granneman, "The Reason Introverts Might 'Think Too Much,'" Introvert, Dear, July 17, 2017, https://introvertdear.com/news/overthinking-introverts-reason/.

Chapter 15 Understand Why You're Not Shy

1. Susan Cain, "Are You Shy, Introverted, Both, or Neither (and Why Does It Matter)?," Quiet Revolution, accessed August 5, 2022, https://www.quietrev.com/are-you-shy-introverted-both-or-neither-and-why-does-it-matter/.
2. Ellen Hendriksen, "The 4 Differences between Introversion and Social Anxiety," Quiet Revolution, accessed August 5, 2022, https://www.quietrev.com/the-4-differences-between-introversion-and-social-anxiety/.

Chapter 16 Get a New Perspective on Joy

1. Timothy Keller, "The Meaning of Shalom in the Bible," New International Version, March 1, 2019, https://www.thenivbible.com/blog/meaning-shalom-bible/.

Chapter 17 Honor Your Need for Rest

1. Saundra Dalton-Smith, *Sacred Rest: Recover Your Life, Renew Your Energy, Restore Your Sanity* (Nashville: FaithWords, 2019).
2. Dalton-Smith, *Sacred Rest*, 201.

Chapter 18 Let Nature Speak to Your Soul

1. Srini Pillay, "How to Use the Benefit of Nature to Reduce Anxiety at Work," Fast Company, January 28, 2020, https://www.fastcompany.com/90455885/how-to-use-the-benefit-of-nature-to-reduce-anxiety-at-work.

Chapter 20 Welcome a New Perspective

1. Amy Palmer, "The Neuroscience of Visualization," *Mind Movies* (blog), accessed August 5, 2022, www.mindmovies.com/blogroll/the-neuroscience-of-visualization.

Chapter 25 Find Your Hiding Place

1. Christy Nockels, "2016 Wrap Up," December 23, 2016, in *The Glorious in the Mundane*, podcast, https://christynockels.com/episode/ep-21-2016-year-end/.
2. Nockels, "2016 Wrap Up."

Chapter 27 Live between Possibility and Potential

1. Elaine Aron, *The Highly Sensitive Person: How to Thrive When the World Over-whelms You* (New York: Harmony Books, 2016), 10.

Chapter 29 Listen to the Gentle Whisper of God

1. 1 Kings 19:11–12.

Holley Gerth is passionate about helping people embrace who they are and become all God created them to be. She's the *Wall Street Journal* bestselling author of many books, including *The Powerful Prupose of Introverts* and *What Your Mind Needs for Anxious Moments*. In addition to being a life coach and former counselor, Holley cofounded the groundbreaking online community (in)courage, which had almost one million page views in its first six months, and cohosts the *More Than Small Talk* podcast. Holley is also wife to Mark, mom to Lovelle, and Nana to Eula and Clement. To connect with Holley and find more tools, resources, and inspiration for introverts, follow her on social media @HolleyGerth or visit Holleygerth.com/introverts.

YOUR INTROVERSION IS **EXACTLY** WHAT YOU NEED TO SUCCEED

If you've ever questioned who you are as an introvert, or if you love, lead, or share life with an introvert, you need this empowering, insightful book.

Я Revell
a division of Baker Publishing Group
www.RevellBooks.com

Available wherever books and ebooks are sold.